Annabel Goldsmith is the daughter of the 8th Marquess of Londonderry. Married first to Mark Birley, who named Annabel's Club in Berkeley Square after her, and then to James Goldsmith, she is the author of a bestselling autobiography, *Annabel: An Unconventional Life* and lives on Ham Common, surrounded by six dogs and numerous grandchildren.

COPPER
A DOG'S LIFE

Annabel Goldsmith

Pen and ink drawings by
India Jane Birley

sphere

SPHERE

First published in Great Britain in 2006 by Sphere
This paperback edition published in 2009 by Sphere

A CIP catalogue record for this book
is available from the British Library.

ISBN 978-0-7515-3820-5

Typeset in Bembo by M Rules
Printed and bound in Great Britain by
Clays Ltd, St Ives plc

Papers used by Sphere are natural, renewable and recyclable
products made from wood grown in sustainable forests and certified
in accordance with the rules of the Forest Stewardship Council.

Mixed Sources
Product group from well-managed
forests and other controlled sources
www.fsc.org Cert no. SGS-COC-004081
© 1996 Forest Stewardship Council
FSC

Sphere
An imprint of
Little, Brown Book Group
100 Victoria Embankment
London EC4Y 0DY

An Hachette Livre UK Company
www.hachettelivre.co.uk

www.littlebrown.co.uk

To all my grandchildren

ACKNOWLEDGEMENTS

I am grateful to the following authors and their books which have provided me with invaluable and interesting information about dogs: Rupert Sheldrake, *Dogs That Know When Their Owners Are Coming Home: And Other Unexplained Powers of Animals*; Bruce Fogle, *The Dog's Mind*; Temple Grandin and Catherine Johnson, *Animals in Translation*; Elizabeth Marshall Thomas, *The Hidden Life of Dogs*; and Jan Fennell, *The Dog Listener*.

I would also like to thank the following people at Little, Brown: Ursula Mackenzie, Emma Stonex, Caroline Hogg and Raquel Leis-Rivera.

Thanks also to my secretary Judith Naish who once again patiently deciphered my handwriting and provided her general sympathetic support, Juliet Nicolson for her friendship and help, and Tom Parker-Bowles for having the brilliant idea of Copper recounting his exploits from heaven.

Last but not least, my thanks to my editor, Rosie de Courcy, without whom I could not have written this book.

CONTENTS

PREFACE

Most people believe that their dogs are special, possessing particular intuition and skills, but once in a while there comes along a truly extraordinary dog capable of almost human exploits. Copper was one of these.

Although I have used poetic licence with the animals' dialogue, most of Copper's story is true. He really did know all the bus routes, how to cross the roads safely by holding up his paw and pretending to be lame, and which was the best pub to eat in. His love life truly was legendary and all of the incidents mentioned were either witnessed by me or by friends who reported them back to me. He even made the national press. One newspaper article, headed 'Dog tired after night at the pub', included quotes from people who had met him on his travels:

The visit to the friendly suburban public house was as regular as clockwork. He always arrived by bus. 'You could set your watch by him,' said locals . . . One former local, Eddie Derbyshire, remembers Copper's visits to the New Inn. 'He was obviously a smart dog,' he said. 'If I had known he was so well connected, I would have made sure he stood his round.'

He certainly stood trial and was lucky to escape with his life; he also made the famous trip to Brighton, although only he knew what really happened there.

I have tried to write this story as he would have liked it to be told, capturing his arrogance, along with his affectionate nature and the aggression he showed towards non-dog lovers. In a way it is my tribute to an amazing dog who will never be forgotten.

Annabel Goldsmith
Ormeley Lodge
January 2006

1

THE BEGINNING

Well, here I am in paradise, looking down on everyone, instead of constantly looking up. It's a funny feeling, I can tell you. I once heard heaven described as the happy hunting ground, and if you like the kind of quiet bliss which I never found for very long on earth, then it is happy all right. But you can forget hunting up here. I pride myself on being an expert; it was one of my very favourite sports. Unfortunately, though, killing things is rather frowned upon here, which is silly when you think that we're all dead anyway. What's a harmless chase between celestial friends? Even if there were to be an accidental killing, we know we'd all float back up again. But the fact is that pretty much all the things which I used to love are out of bounds. We are on a higher plane now.

My mother used to say that only dull dogs are bored, and although I know she was right, sometimes I can't help feeling a little wistful about my life on earth. I did have so much fun, you know. And although I pushed my luck again and again, I always tried to do it in style, and have been told – forgive me if this sounds conceited – that it was usually with charm. I suppose I was what you would call a charming rogue. I was certainly a ladies' man, but we'll come back to that.

I was born one bitterly cold day, when the frost lay bone-hard on the ground, breath drifted in the air like smoke and the trees were sharp and black against the sky. Many of the winters which I experienced later were damp and still, with the clouds seeming to hang just above your head, like a chill grey blanket. People used to talk about being under the weather, and that's literally how it felt. But the winter of my birth wasn't like that at all. It was crisp and high and clear; in spite of all our mother's precautions, we were often cold and water was hard to come by.

My first memories are of my mother and of lying snuggled up to the roughness and warmth of her fur. There were ten of us: puppies of all different colours, from black to fawn, from brindle to pied. And then there was me, a deep reddish brown, 'Like a little fox, or even autumn leaves,' said my mother as she was washing me. 'Reminds me of your father.' Like all puppies, we were born with our eyes closed; our mother did not leave us until our eyes had opened. Her extraordinary patience as we fought and jostled for the first teat is one of my abiding memories of her.

I am not sure exactly whereabouts we were born, but I know that it was in a broken-down shed, surrounded by a rough patch of land, near a bus station. I can remember foxes and feral cats out hunting, whose smell I hated even then. And grey squirrels, which my mother described as 'Rats with bushy tails, fair game for any self-respecting dog.' You see, my mother may have been living rough, but she had very high standards. She had fallen on hard times but she knew how things should be done and she was determined that we should know too. I can honestly say that what she told us and the tips she gave us before we were parted for ever were the basis of my success in later life, and I often had cause to remember them during the many adventures which I am going to recount.

First of all she explained that we were cross-bred – mongrel was on her list of banned words – and that this had advantages and disadvantages in the world of men. It would make us more intelligent, resourceful and resilient than pedigree dogs, but without a loving home and an owner to protect us we were more likely to be treated with cruelty, shot at by gamekeepers like vermin or even drowned as unwanted puppies. Above all, we must never ever slink or cringe; subservience would be treated with contempt. 'Always carry yourselves with pride,' she said. 'A touch of arrogance never goes amiss.'

She told us about our father, an Alsatian-terrier cross who could never be tamed: a legendary fighter with lupine blood and a wonderful nose, but restless and unwise. What happened to him? we wanted to know. 'Run over by a car.

Chasing some silly bitch on heat, I expect,' our mother replied contemptuously. We didn't really understand one word of it then: bitches, on heat, cars. It sounded like non-sense but, later on, when my own adventures began, I remembered my father and devised a strategy for dealing with roads and traffic which, even though I say it myself, was quite brilliant. I'll tell you about it in due course.

My mother believed in dignified behaviour. She also understood all about people, because at one time in her life she had been owned by some. She said that there were things people liked about dogs and things they didn't. They did not like us stealing their food or biting other humans, and in par-ticular, weeing – or worse – in their houses. Humans also disliked whining, pointless barking and too much licking of hands and faces. However, they did very much like their houses being protected, in which case we could bark all we wanted. They also loved playfulness in their dogs; some-thing like rolling over on your back usually went down well because it made them laugh.

'You have to use your imagination,' our mother advised, 'get it right and you won't go wrong.'

My eldest brother didn't like the sound of this much. 'I won't do it,' he said. 'I'm going to live wild and free like the foxes.'

'Wild or tame, free or not, there are some things you cannot change, and you'd better understand what they are,' replied my mother. 'Now listen carefully, all of you. In this world of ours there are two kinds of animal. There are the hunters and the hunted. There are fight animals and there are flight animals. In the first group, the largest and fiercest is man. In the second, the largest and most fleet is the horse. We dogs are hunters and fighters. We can co-exist peacefully with others in our group, such as foxes, badgers and human beings, or we can fight them. Either way, it is human beings who rule our world. You must understand that, my children, or you will not survive.'

But this particular brother of mine was stubborn. No, he said, he was going to live rough and lead a great pack of dogs which no human on earth would dare to challenge. My mother sighed. 'Time for some education, then. Sounds as if you're going to need all the help you can get.' She went on, 'Who can tell me what a dog's most powerful weapon is?'

'Teeth, teeth! It's our teeth!' shouted my two rowdiest sisters at once.

'No,' she said, 'it isn't. Teeth are very important, of course, and it is true that a toothless dog is no use to anyone. But your most powerful weapon, puppies, is your eye. The very first thing you must do when facing an opponent, or someone who wants to dominate you, is to stare him down. First he will look away, then turn his head aside. Finally, when he yawns you'll know you've won. He has submitted, and he yawns to show that he's embarrassed.'

I am not sure how many of us believed her then, and certainly I was doubtful. We were much more excited by chasing and pouncing, biting and scratching, as we rolled each other over and over on the ground. Staring each other out sounded like an awful waste of good fighting time. For you see, these were happy days. We were never hungry, thirsty or bored; although we were living wild and were sometimes cold, we felt safe.

But one day everything changed. Our mother went out foraging – scavenging was another word she hated – and did not come back. As the hours passed, we became restless and frightened. She had never left us for so long. As night fell we forgot our mother's warnings about keeping quiet at dusk. My brothers barked, my sisters howled and I whimpered quietly to myself.

'What's all this noise?' The voice was harsh, the eyes cold and clear: the biggest dog fox I had ever seen was standing in our shed, his brush twitching slightly from side to side, looking as though he wanted to devour the lot of us. We shrank and cowered; he stalked closer. Desperately I fixed my eyes on his. What was it exactly that my mother had said? Stare him down? But I could not hold the gaze of those wild, light eyes for more than a few seconds, and it was I, not he, who turned aside.

'Wise pup,' he said drily. 'Where's your mother?'

'We don't know, sir. We're on our own and very hungry.'

'Hmm. Sorry to hear that. I'll see if there's any word on the street. Someone may know something.'

Two more long and lonely days and nights passed before our friend returned.

'I'm sorry, pups. Nothing. Not a sign. Not a word. We're all sorry. She was a fine dog.'

'Oh sir, whatever can we do?'

'Don't know. I'd like to help you, but your mother chose a funny time of year to whelp. None of my vixens can foster you for a couple of months yet.' And with that he was gone, a russet shadow slipping out of our lives as noiselessly as he had come.

Our case seemed hopeless. We were starving, we were cold and very, very frightened. The unearthly shriek of vixens in search of a mate, the lonely cry of a hunting owl and the screams of tomcats fighting to the death: these were the sounds which haunted our nights now. These and visions of what might have happened to our mother. Trapped in a storm drain? Drowned? Fatally injured? Captured? Probably we would never know. Without her we were in terrible danger.

In every litter of puppies there are the strong and there are the weak. Ours was no exception. One of my sisters was now causing me a lot of worry. My mother had always said this one was delicate and now she began, day by day, to slip away from us. I did what I know my mother would have wanted. I kept her close and washed her, warming her with my body, keeping her blood circulating with the rough, steady movements of my tongue. I thought I could feel her breathing getting shallower. I whispered to her, 'Don't go, little sister, don't go. Mother's coming back. Just hang on a bit longer.' But I had no power to hold her. I felt her body stiffen and her fur grow cold. Her spirit was the first to leave us but I knew that as surely as night follows day, one by one, we would all die too.

I don't know exactly how much time passed then, as we lay huddled in that half-sleeping, half-waking state which often accompanies extreme hunger and cold. But suddenly the broken door of the shed was wrenched aside and a large figure of some kind stood silhouetted against the light. Had I but known it, this was my first sighting of a male human being.

'What the hell have we got here?' he said and came closer to have a look. 'Jim,' he shouted, 'come over here!'

Another huge figure appeared by his side. He stared at us and said, 'Poor little blighters. They've been abandoned by some bastard.'

They both looked down at us, obscuring the light from the door. The first man spoke again. 'Tell you what, I'll take them to my brother Bill. He's got a butcher's shop in Hounslow. He loves mutts of all kinds.'

The man called Jim sniggered. 'What's he going to do with them? Hang them up by their tails in the window and put up a sign saying "Fresh puppy meat"?' They both laughed. This is it, I thought. This is the end.

The next moment we were all gathered up and bundled into a van. You will understand, of course, that then I didn't know exactly what this thing was. It looked and sounded like a growling, shuddering animal, but a very odd animal with no head or tail. However, our mother had given us a bit of instruction about cars and the buses which came and went from the shelter near our shed and we soon put two and two together. To this day, accustomed as I became to public transport, I can still remember that journey. The jostling and bumping, the noise, the smell of diesel and above all the sheer terror of not knowing what would become of us: it is all as vivid as if it happened yesterday.

After what seemed a lifetime, the van stopped and we were bundled up once more. Light dazzled our eyes. The babble of human voices assaulted our ears. One by one we were lowered into a pen lined with paper. Someone placed a bowl of water and a plate of raw minced meat beside us but we were too weak to eat or drink and by and by we each sank back into a coma, half-way between life and death.

I don't like to dwell now on what might have happened if the butcher's wife had not taken a hand in our fate. But she did. She saw that we were severely dehydrated and under-nourished. She got rid of the meat and the water and instead patiently fed us by hand with warm bread and milk. Little by little, hour after painful hour, our strength began to return. My mother had been right about cross-breeds. We were strong. We would survive.

I suppose that we had been in the butcher's shop for about a fortnight when once again my fortunes changed. We had watched people come and go: talking, laughing, arguing. We had begun to understand the rudiments of human speech and to tell male from female, adult from child. We had feasted on scraps and chewed on bones. We were warm and well-fed. But, to be candid, we were bored. We needed a wider world. Now, I don't know about you, but personally I have always found that just when you need a new road a path miraculously opens up before you. And that is what happened now.

I was romping in an idle kind of way with my eldest

brother (who by now had changed his tune about wanting to lead a pack of wild dogs and rather fancied himself as a butcher's guard dog) when a very tall woman walked into the shop. She spotted us at once and came straight over to our pen. I would like to tell you that what happened next was a well-laid plan inspired by my mother's advice, but the fact is that I was accidentally lying on my back with all four paws in the air, because my brother had rolled me over. I felt very slightly silly. But the tall woman bent over me without looking at any of the others. She picked me up and cradled me in her hands, gazing into my face. I gave her an experimental little lick and, looking back, I think that is what did it.

'I love this little copper-coloured thing,' she said. 'I would like this one.'

The next thing I knew I was carried out of the shop and into a car. Behind me I could hear my brothers and sisters calling goodbye. This journey was quite different from the one in the van and I began to drift off to sleep on a warm lap. Everything felt strange and I did not know what was happening but I had a feeling of safety and comfort, as if I was lying against my mother.

When I awoke, I was being carried into a building far bigger than anything I had seen before. There was a lot of human noise and children gazing at me. One child in particular, a girl with very long hair called Jemima, picked me up and carried me into a huge garden. Oh there was so much grass! I had never seen anything like it. No dust. No buses. Overcome, I stretched my legs out, had a good sniff and peed where I stood. Well, you've never heard such a commotion.

Everyone spoke at once: 'Isn't he clever – good boy! He knew what to do.' Of course I didn't have the slightest idea what they were all talking about, but I was so happy to have done the right thing that I couldn't resist having a little run around the grass – and promptly fell over. Everyone laughed, then Jemima picked me up, singing softly under her breath, took me upstairs in the house and cuddled and fussed over me until I fell asleep. I had arrived at Ormeley Lodge.

2

ORMELEY LODGE

The first few weeks after my arrival were very bewilder-
ing for me. Used to a rickety old shed and then to the
butcher's shop, I had never even seen a house before, let
alone been inside one, and Ormeley Lodge wasn't just any
old house. To my puppy eyes it was the most confusing
jumble of doors and stairs, of tables and chairs, not to men-
tion people of all shapes and sizes. From where I sit now,
though, I can tell you that it was very beautiful but not
formal, big without being grand, and despite all the special
pictures and furniture it was always cosy.

The human pack took some sorting out in my mind. Top
dog was Jimmy, but he spent a lot of time away, hunting and
foraging. I've got a feeling that he was rather like my own

father: a wanderer, not content to be in one place for any length of time. Next in line was my rescuer, whom everyone in the house called Mum. Then came the people who worked for her and looked after us animals.

Isabel and Arnaldo cooked, Maria made up my basket every day and fed me and Mimi looked after Mum's children. Like the best dominant pack-dogs, Mimi was strict but fair and we all loved her. I think we knew that, even when she was being fierce, it was our happiness that she cared about. She also made the best cup of tea in the world. Personally I never was much of a tea drinker, but some of the other dogs who joined me later at Ormeley were very partial to it and would cajole Mum into pouring a little into her saucer for them. No one could make it like Mimi, they said. It was putting the milk in first that did it.

Mum had had two litters of children. With her first husband, Mark, there was Rupert, Robin and India Jane. With Jimmy there was Zac, Jemima and Ben. Jemima was the reason that I came to Ormeley. She had been promised a puppy for passing the exam which would take her through to her next school. Jemima was very clever by human standards, but here's an odd thing which I've noticed: human beings are ridiculously interested in reading and writing. Jemima always had her 'nose in a book' – that is, when she wasn't riding her pony – and Mum made quite a fuss about the business of exams. But as any dog will tell you, reading and writing things on paper is not the only way to get on in life. Reading *each other* is what you want to practise. I could tell you, for example, from the moment she opened her eyes in the morning till the second she switched her light out at night, what kind of mood Mum was in and who was making her happy or unhappy.

I sometimes heard a lot of nonsense talked about how dogs are mind-readers or – even sillier – clairvoyant. And all this just because they know when their owners are coming back from holiday. People were amazed that when the Queen was due to arrive at her country house, all her labradors started barking. Well, of course they did. All they had to do was watch the behaviour of the people around them. I always knew when Mum or Jemima were only leaving the room for a moment, in which case it wouldn't be worth my while to move, or when they had departed for good, when of course I would follow them. By the time I was a grown dog, I can tell you I knew everything about everyone in that house.

There was one human activity, however, which did teach me a lot and that was watching television. In particular there was a film called *The Belstone Fox*, which the children watched over and over again. It was about an orphan fox who was reared in captivity and made friends with a hound. Because it always had the children in floods of tears, I would snuggle up to them and push my wet nose under the nearest hand to cheer them up. 'Oh Copper,' they would say, 'oh Copper, it's so sad. Why couldn't he just have stayed indoors where he was safe, instead of going off hunting?'

Because it was in his nature, I thought. Just as it is in mine. But I tried not to think about that. I was warm and happy and loved. I had everything that my mother ever dreamed of but could never have. I tried to be grateful.

There were two other dogs at Ormeley Lodge when I arrived: sheepdogs called Flora and Tessa. But unlike me – or indeed any of the other dogs who were to come afterwards – they did not actually live in the house, but outside in a kennel of their own.

Later on I understood that Mum felt bad about Flora and Tessa: that she was not able to love them as much as she did me and all the other dogs who were to follow me into her life. I know she wondered if perhaps this was because they were already six months old when they arrived and closely attached to each other, less willing to bond with any human owner. It troubled her that she hadn't chosen them herself; they had just arrived one day out of the blue, tucked into a cardboard box, a present from her first husband. And, on top of this, Mum's second litter were still very young; she was as preoccupied with them as my mother had been with us and guarded them as closely. She had nothing in the way of time or love to spare for a brace of collie puppies.

There have been so many times in my life, both then and later, when I wished I had the power of human speech. If I had been able to speak, I would have explained that although Mum was partly right she had overlooked one very important thing. Flora and Tessa were sheepdogs. Now, I don't mean by this that no sheepdog can be close to its owner. Far from it. Rather that sheepdogs are born and bred to work.

And I mean *work*: running for miles across open country in the blazing heat of the summer sun or the freezing wind and lashing rain of a hill-farm winter. They can jump a five-bar gate or swim a rushing river; they can lie as still as stone, holding a hundred head of sheep in one place; or they can twist and turn like snakes as they move the flock from hill to valley.

'How do you do it?' I asked. 'Hold them in one place, I mean? I can understand about chasing them from one field to the next, but making them all stand still . . .'

'It's the eye, of course,' said Flora.

'What eye?' The eye my mother had talked about?

'The sheepdog eye,' said Tessa. 'The long stare. It comes from our ancestors. The further a dog gets away from wolves in his breeding, the less he can do it. Those silly things with squashed faces – oh you know, Flora – what are they called?'

'Boxers?'

'No, no, not them. Though they'd be no good either. King Charles; yes, that's it. King Charles spaniels. They've got no eye at all. Couldn't outstare a mouse.'

There and then I resolved to ask the sheepdogs to teach me everything they knew. And so they did. Not just about rounding up sheep and other herd animals, or jumping and swimming, but other things which my mother would have explained if she had had the time. They taught me how to clean a wound with my own saliva, how to use the digestive properties of grass or the droppings of grass-eaters like sheep, deer and horses, to cleanse the gut. I learned how to mark my territory and to recognise the signatures of other hunters:

the rank, heavy scent of fox; the sour, thin smell of cat; and the overpowering stench of badger, the meat which no dog will touch. Flora and Tessa taught me all this and more. I adored them but their sadness in the end made me sad and because of this I began to move away from them. It's not something I'm proud of and I don't like to talk about their death even now. But I was younger and sillier then.

I had much to get used to in those early days. The worst thing was being on my own at night. I had been accustomed to all kinds of hardship but not to loneliness and at first I cried for the mother I had lost, for my brothers and sisters whom I would never see again and for the little one I had not been able to save. I even cried for that tumbledown old shed we had called home.

'For heaven's sake, stop that dreadful racket,' said a cross voice one night. 'Whatever's the matter?'

It was Jessie, the small black cat who lived at Ormeley. Despite her size, she seemed to give herself tremendous airs and I wasn't sure that I liked her. My mother never had a kind word to say about the feral cats who hunted on our rough patch of land. Jessie wasn't feral, but she was certainly a cat.

'Shove over,' she said now. 'I'll purr you to sleep.'

I don't think my mother could have known about purring or she would have changed her mind about cats. It is quite simply the most relaxing, contented sound in the world and within minutes I was dead to the world.

After that we became great sparring partners. Sometimes I would tease her until she spat at me and slapped me with

20

her paw. Occasionally I would invite her to join me in my basket, luxuriating in the praise this elicited from the family, but as soon as anyone left the room I bared my teeth and pushed her out. It was good fun.

Over the next few months I never tired of hearing how intelligent and alert my face was and how my rapidly sprouting beard gave me an air of dignity. I was beginning to grow long agile legs and a tail that curled up at the end. It did not take me long to explore every inch of the garden, to cock my leg against every tree, bush and piece of garden furniture. I no longer had to squat to pee. This marking of territory, as I knew from the collies, is a very important aspect of male dog ritual and I now regarded the garden as exclusively mine. Now that I could manage the stairs, I also considered every room in the house as my property but cocking your leg against the curtains or a chair was strictly forbidden as I found to my cost.

I had grown to love Mum and the children and tried to please them by retrieving balls and sticks and, in the summer, joining them in the swimming pool, chasing them round and round, while they shrieked in pretend terror. Strictly speaking the swimming was not a chore – it was something I enjoyed. Occasionally I know I went too far, especially when there were a lot of children running round the pool. Every now and again I couldn't resist a playful nip at their ankles.

The truth of the matter was that I had my father's hunting blood in me and I longed to chase just about everything that moved. Sometimes the longing rose up in me like a joyous fever and I would yearn to run with the great herds of deer which roamed Richmond Park. At other times I would be consumed by a kind of fierce hunger and then I would have hunted to kill if I could.

Mum allowed me to chase and kill squirrels and I enjoyed that, but the prey of which I dreamed, night and day, was not animal but human. Shocking, I know, but there it is. Some dogs can't stand small children, or even other dogs. But for me it was joggers. I didn't mind women running past me. It was the men I hated. Something to do with their white, hairy legs.

I am sorry to say that this caused quite a bit of friction between Mum and me. Whenever Jimmy came home, he would laugh and say, 'Quite right, Copper. Any dog worth his salt should bite joggers.'

But Mum, who was usually the first to get the joke in any situation, did not laugh. She saw that my obsession could end up being my undoing.

Then another idea began to grip me too. I wanted to be free to come and go from Ormeley like Jessie did. I decided to ask her advice. She was not encouraging: 'First of all, Copper, you can't jump high enough to get over the wall and, secondly, you haven't got a clue about traffic. You've got no idea how many animals get killed out there on the roads.' Oh yes I have, I thought. Father, for one. But Jessie went on, 'Just forget about it. Truly, Copper, you must. Promise me. Mum takes you on long walks, doesn't she? And frankly, although we all know you're a complete nuisance, for some reason she loves you. It would break her heart – and Jemima's come to that – if you got squashed out there.'

But I wasn't listening. 'OK, so I can't jump as high as you, but what about getting through the gates?'

No, she thought that was a non-starter as well. All right then, I thought, if she wouldn't help me I would just have to work it out for myself.

The most important and also the most beautiful room in Ormeley Lodge was Mum's bedroom. This is where she wrote letters, talked on the telephone to her friends and watched television with the children. I loved it and would sleep on the sofa there in front of the fireplace whenever I could, or whenever Jemima didn't take me off to her bed. The room had two great windows which stretched from floor to ceiling and at night, while Mum slept, I would sometimes stand looking out. At full moon you could see right up to the end of the garden. Hour after hour I watched, looking to see where the foxes, cleverest of all the night hunters, got in and out.

By day I would scour every inch of the wall which ran round the outside of the garden. I felt sure that there must be a weakness somewhere, a place where I could make a hole. Maybe I could dig underneath. I knew that badgers and rabbits could make tunnels, so why couldn't I? The more I thought about it, in fact, the more brilliant the idea seemed. The main thing was to discover a place where I would not be seen. I had already got into trouble for digging under the garden door. And at length I found it: a spot perfectly screened by shrubs and by the long grass which grew underneath them. Here I could work in peace, inching my way, day by day, towards freedom.

At first it was difficult to find a time to be undisturbed by my loving little owner but presently I realised that early morning, before everyone was properly awake, and late summer nights while it was still light were perfect tunnelling times. I learned to sneak out of the house through Jessie's cat flap as soon as it got light but it was on just such a morning that all my plans crumbled to dust and I got the fright of my life.

It was one of those summer dawns, when the mist is lying just above the ground before the sun has burned it off. The owls had stopped hunting and the songbirds were beginning to stir. I trotted as quietly as I could up the garden, not wanting to alert those noisy devils the blackbirds. They can set up a dreadful racket if they are surprised and I didn't want Jemima to wake up and find me gone. I was getting in deeper and deeper under the wall and I was gripped by a perfect fever of excitement. I hadn't the slightest sense of danger that wonderful summer morning. I was on my way to freedom, and nothing could stop me now. If that sounds heartless, it isn't meant to be. I did love Mum and the children, and all the comforts of Ormeley, but there was wild blood in me and the outside world called incessantly, giving me no peace until I could be part of its great adventures.

I crept through the grass under the branches of the shrubs which hid my secret and crawled into the mouth of my tunnel. I was digging for dear life, making tremendous headway, when all of a sudden the ground disappeared beneath my front paws and I found myself tumbling head-long into space. Down and down I fell until at last I came to rest on what seemed to be the floor of a huge cavern. More shocked than hurt, I looked around me, my eyes gradually getting used to the dim light.

There were chambers and passages leading off the main den in all directions. From one of these there now appeared the oddest looking animal but one whose strong smell I recognised instantly. This badger had a narrow black-and-white striped head with small slanting eyes and a long nose, thick muscular shoulders and a wide, soft body covered in brownish-grey fur. The eyes gleamed at me suspiciously. Then a voice, gruff but not unkind, said 'Now then, young 'un. Where have Mum and Dad got to?'

I was about to say that my mother and father were dead when I realised that the badger had made a mistake.

'It's not your turn here yet, you know,' she went on, 'not till we're finished with it. You'd better go back the way you came. The other badgers aren't very keen on foxes.'

The collies had impressed on me that it was a very bad idea to get on the wrong side of badgers. They were short-sighted and looked ungainly but had a better sense of smell than foxes and dogs put together. And they were extremely dangerous fighters.

'What's the whelp doing in our sett?' This voice was a good deal less friendly than the first one; this badger much bigger.

'Lost his way, by the look of it. He'll be going now.'

But I should have known it wasn't going to be that easy. 'Smells like a dog to me.'

'Dog!' They spoke now with one voice and moved towards me, clumsy but unmistakably threatening.

I did not know what to do or where to turn. I couldn't remember what badgers were supposed to eat. Did they like meat? Worse still, did they like puppy meat? I admit that I panicked. Wriggling ingratiatingly, half-whining, half-whimpering, with my belly to the earth in an apologetic way that my mother might not altogether have liked, I explained how I came to be there.

'All right, my dear,' said the first badger at last. 'I can tell you mean no harm and I wouldn't like one of our cubs to get lost like that. My mate will show you out.'

'Shove you out, more like,' growled her mate and pushed me unceremoniously back up one of the passages. I emerged, panting with anxiety, into the light of day, only to be met by the most petrifying noise and even more terrifying sight. A screeching, hissing, yowling ball of black fur with blazing eyes. Jessie. But a Jessie I had never seen before. Gone was my languid, purring friend. Instead I faced a huge spitting tornado of a cat, infuriated because I had blundered in on the final stages of her last hunting stalk of the night.

'Copper, you half-witted idiot!' she shrieked. 'What the hell do you think you are doing?'

'Digging a tunnel,' I said, 'but then . . .'

'Are you mad?' said Jessie, interrupting me incredulously. 'First you want to hurl yourself over the wall, under the wheels of the first car that comes along. Now you've declared war on the foxes and badgers who control all the tunnels along here. You're going to get yourself killed and, frankly, I'm not sure that I care any more.'

'Jessie,' I began again humbly, 'I'm sorry. Truly I am. But you must see it isn't fair. You can jump and climb your way out of here whenever you want. Those foxes and badgers are even luckier. They can make their own secret roads.' I did not dare admit now that I had already had a nasty scare underground.

But Jessie was not to be placated. 'Copper, you're a lunatic and that's all there is to it. I'm washing my paws of you.'

Only she didn't, of course. Instead she drove me mad by watching every single move I made.

3

BRANCHING OUT

One of Jessie's favourite places was on top of the wall beside the large wooden gates through which everyone came and went to Ormeley. She used to snooze there, curled up in the sun, often with one eye half open to see what was going on. I discovered that if I sat on the window seat on the first-floor landing I too could have an excellent view of all the comings and goings.

Postmen, milkmen, dustmen: I watched them all and noted the times of their arrivals and departures. I was looking for the moment when the gates would stay open for a while and I could slip out unobserved.

The various deliverymen and Steve the gardener, who arrived every morning at eight, were all very careful to shut the gates behind them. But the dustmen, who had to back their huge lorry into the yard once a week, looked more promising. It took them at least five minutes to manoeuvre the lorry, open the back and then hurl into it the quantities of rubbish and food which got thrown away at Ormeley each week. What rich pickings my mother would have found in those leftovers!

The other advantage of the dustmen's arrival lay in the fact that they came early in the morning, before the children were up and about to interfere with my plans. The trick was to wait until they were throwing bags into the back and then to slip out between the gatepost and the front wheel of the lorry. Some time after the failure of my tunnelling, I decided to give it a go.

Out through the back door, into the yard; no one seemed in the least interested in what I was up to. Even Jessie was oblivious, curled up in her basket with her tail over her nose, after a busy night's hunting. I sniffed at the wheels of the dustcart as if I hadn't a care in the world then, quick as a flash, dashed out towards the gates.

'Mind that dog!' The shout came from Steve, unexpectedly appearing in the yard from the garden. I could have made a run for it but I would probably have been quickly caught and brought back. In any case, it was the freedom of the open road that I craved, not the hunted existence of a fugitive on the run. I turned back, tail wagging, and allowed myself to be shooed into the house again.

'Ha ha,' said Jessie sarcastically from her basket, apparently wide awake now. 'That'll teach you.'

Oh no it won't, I thought. But I didn't say anything. I was beginning to learn that there was no point in arguing with a cat who was as conceited as she was selfish.

My life settled back into its usual routine: walks on Ham Common and in Richmond Park, and trips down to Manor Farm, where the children kept their ponies. Manor Farm was a higgledy-piggledy hive of activity: there were ponies being led up and down, stables being mucked out, buckets filled and emptied, tack cleaned and so many, many smells. The sweet scent of new hay and the musty smell of old straw mingled with manure, sweat and the tang of leather. Half-wild cats slept in the barn or watched patiently for the rats which sometimes scuttled about in the shadows. Molly, the stable dog, would become the first great love of my life. She was not only quite beautiful – a black long-haired collie-cross – but also great fun to play with. Together we ran, we barked, we pounced and raced, while Zac and Jemima groomed and tacked-up the ponies. They then plodded round and round the outdoor arena, being shouted at from time to time by their instructor. Dull work, but they seemed to like it.

Every weekend we would load up the ponies and drive to a horse show. In theory this should have been great fun: a big open field, plenty to see and smell, endless scraps of food dropped on the ground for an opportunist like me to snack on. But I hated those horse shows for one simple reason. I had to be kept on a lead the whole time.

'It's against a dog's instinct,' I said one day to Jemima's pony April.

'Instinct!' she snorted. 'It's against *my* instinct to stand caged up in a dark stable, or to go out alone across country without the herd to protect me, or to jump those silly striped poles. Come to that, it's against *my* instinct to carry Jemima on my back at all. In the wild, if you've got something on your back it's because you are about to die. You think about that, young Copper.'

I did think about it and I also listened to the other ponies as they munched and gossiped and dozed in their stables at Manor Farm. The truth was that, although they were grateful for food and occasionally for shelter, for the most part they merely tolerated a way of life that had been designed with human beings in mind and bore no resemblance to what ponies really wanted or needed. They wanted to be outside in all weathers, shaded by trees from the heat of the sun or backed up against a hedge in the wet. They needed grass, water and fresh air, and they needed to be able to see and touch each other: nibbling, scratching and grooming. Isolated in dark stables, tied up by headcollars, over-heated in rugs and bandages: they endured it all but it was not the life of their choice.

I had reluctantly begun to accept that I would never have the life of my choice either, when something happened at Ormeley that changed my landscape for ever. The old gates, which opened and closed by hand, were replaced by ones which, at the touch of a button from inside the house, opened slowly to allow cars and people in or out and then hovered ajar for a few precious seconds each time before closing. For a few days I watched, waiting for my chance. And one never-to-be-forgotten morning, it came.

A large van, carrying pieces of furniture, turned up, but because it was too big for the courtyard the removal men had to carry the furniture in through the gates from outside. Apart from Jessie, lying in her usual place on top of the garden wall, no one was looking at me. As the gates hovered, I sprinted through them.

'Madness,' hissed Jessie, as I made for the road. 'You're heading for disaster.'

But I didn't care. My heart raced. My blood sang. The world lay before me. I would not waste it.

I sauntered slowly along the pavement that ran under the trees beside the road, heading for Ham Common. This part of the road was quite quiet but I could see that up ahead of me, where a bigger road ran from right to left, cars, lorries and motorbikes were flashing to and fro. Here was danger. I knew that full well. I had no intention of ending up like my father: life snuffed out in a moment of recklessness. I had to learn how to cross roads safely.

As soon as I arrived at the main road, I sat down to watch how people managed to get across from one side to the other. I knew already what Mum and I usually did. We came to the lights and then, when the traffic stopped, we crossed. But because I had always been on a lead I had not needed to work out for myself how the traffic stopped and started. This is what I had to figure out now.

In fact it was not very difficult on this occasion. Later on I knew I would have to come up with a way of getting traffic to stop for me but on this first day there were plenty of people coming and going. I attached myself to a group, following their every move, until I had safely arrived on the other side of the road on Ham Common.

Mum and I had often been here together so I knew my way around pretty well and I had several friends who I used to meet up with on our walks. There was Nina; mysterious and capricious. She was a pie-dog, born in Bombay and brought over to England by her loving owner, having had to endure six months of quarantine.

In India, people believe in reincarnation and pie-dogs are reputed to be the reincarnation of punished princesses, which explained Nina's regal bearing and slightly haughty demeanour. Her markings of black, brown and white were bold and beautiful, and she held her head at a proud angle. She could be either your best friend or your worst enemy, both loving and vicious, depending on her mood. I liked her because of all the dogs I had met so far, she was by far the naughtiest; as far as bad behaviour was concerned, she put me in the shade with her lawlessness.

However, the friend I liked best was a dog called Bungle, whose mistress, Veronica, came once a week to do something to Mum's hair. I never understood quite what, as it always looked exactly the same at the end as it had when she started. But I was happy when she came because she always brought Bungle to play with me in the garden. Bungle was a little black Scottie, or Scottish terrier. And my goodness, did we ever hear about the Scottish bit. Although he was born and bred in the north of England and had never set foot in Scotland in his life, he was very proud of his ancestry to the point of affecting a slight Scots burr when he spoke. I reckoned he had picked it up from watching television.

'My kennel name is The Bungle of MacIntyre of That Ilk,' he informed me in the slightly pompous, hushed voice he used when talking about his pedigree.

'Oh really,' I said, wondering why you'd be pleased to be called The Bungle of anywhere at all.

'Yes,' he went on. 'An ancestor of mine was on the boat with Bonnie Prince Charlie. It's a shame you're a mongrel, Copper. You don't really have any history.'

'Well,' I said, thoroughly nettled, 'for a start I'm not a mongrel, I'm *cross-bred* and, secondly, I'm descended on my father's side directly from wolves.'

'Oh, so am I,' said Bungle earnestly. 'I'm a descendant of the wolf. All dogs are.'

I burst out laughing. Anything less like a wolf than Bungle, with his short little legs and square body, was hard to imagine.

'All right then,' he said, offended now, 'tell me about these parents of yours.'

And so I did but, as I talked, I could feel myself getting sadder, my high spirits ebbing a little.

'And then we never saw her again.' My voice faltered and I fell silent. I didn't want to see the pity and condescension on Bungle's face so I turned my head away.

'Copper. I say, Copper.' Reluctantly I looked at him. I saw not pity, not condescension, but the steady, shrewd gaze of true friendship. And, more than that, I saw in his wise, loyal face something steely, almost excited.

'Copper, old fellow. You shouldn't leave it there, you know.'

'What do you mean?'

'I mean that you should find your mother. Or at least find out what happened to her.' I gawped at him. 'You don't know for sure that she's dead. All you do know, from your friend the fox, is that she vanished without trace. Now, if you were to ask *me*, I'd say the most likely thing is that she got shut in somewhere. She's probably back on the street by now.'

I don't think that Bungle had the least idea what an astounding thing he had just said. For suddenly, with those few words, he had given my whole yearning for freedom a shape and a purpose.

'Bungle,' I said, 'you're right. I apologise. Pedigree is everything. You're a genius.'

He wriggled appreciatively. 'I'll keep my ears cocked. You never know what I might hear on my walks.'

And now, on my first precious day of freedom, there was Bungle himself, ambling about off the lead, while his mistress sat gossiping on a bench under the trees. We greeted each other in our usual manner with a great deal of bottom-sniffing and tail-wagging, which in Bungle's case meant his whole compact little body wagged.

'What are you doing out on your own?' said Bungle, cocking his leg on the nearest bench and sending the earth flying as he scratched the ground with his back legs.

'I've escaped for the day,' I told him, full of self-impor-
tance.

If Bungle was impressed, he was careful not to show it.
'What on earth for?' he asked, putting his black head to one
side. 'Why do you want to do a silly thing like that when
your mistress is so nice to you?'

'I've taken your advice. I'm going to see if I can find out
what happened to my family.'

Bungle was aghast. 'But Copper,' he stammered, 'I didn't
mean go off on your *own* and do it. I meant just keep your
ears open for news. Mum takes you about a lot with the
ponies and everything.'

I looked at him pityingly. 'I'll never get anywhere like
that. There's a lot of ground to cover. People to see. Places to
go.' But I knew that he would not understand. And now
here was Veronica, tartan lead in hand.

'Come on, Bungle. Time to go home,' she said. 'Oh
hello, Copper. Where's your mum, then?'

Bungle not being a real goody-goody at heart, and true
friend that he was, instantly distracted her by trying to give
her the slip. But Veronica was too quick for him and I
watched him being dragged off reluctantly, his head twisted
backwards in my direction.

I was sorry to see him go because I would have liked to
play with him and although I had told him that I was on a
mission to find my family, it wasn't strictly true on this most
thrilling first day of freedom. I just wanted to have fun and
to explore the new boundaries of my world. I could see the
pond gleaming tantalisingly up ahead of me; Bungle and I

had often discussed catching the ducks that swam there and had planned a most brilliant pincer movement to secure our prey. Now he was gone, I would have to have a go on my own. Thanks to Mum and the children, I was, at least, an excellent swimmer.

I ran on until I came to the pond and, much to my delight, I saw several ducks and a pair of swans floating majestically around. This was too much to resist. I leapt into the pond and gave chase. Well, you have never heard such a racket: frantic quacking from the ducks; hissing from some geese, which had suddenly appeared from nowhere; and shouts from mothers with small children, who were feeding the ducks with bits of bread.

I managed to snaffle some of the bread before it hit the water, but it was a duck that I really wanted. I swam after a particularly fat one with a large crust in its beak. I had just managed to grab its tail feathers when a furious man, who I had previously spotted sitting on a bench surrounded by pigeons and seagulls, rose to his feet and ran to the pond shouting, 'Get out of that pond, you filthy cur!'

He was scarlet in the face and also had fat, red legs tightly encased in shorts. At first I ignored him, but he waded into the water and tried to grab my tail. Reluctantly deciding that I had better come out, I shook myself and soaked his legs and his bulging stomach. By this time his face, contorted with rage, had turned an odd shade of purple and he raised his stick and struck me across my bottom. In return I grabbed the stick in my mouth, pretending it was a game, but this plan backfired. He wrenched the stick free, gave me another whack and shouted 'Clear off!' You will not be surprised to hear that I was tempted to bite him but thought better of it in the end and ran off. It was my first encounter with the bad side of humans. Time to retreat.

We dogs cannot tell the time as exactly as humans do; we know that dawn means get up and go, dusk means sleep and hunger means dinner time. I was not sure where it had got to in the day and, although all my exertions had made me feel peckish, I was not yet ready to return home. I could smell something quite delicious coming from a building on the corner of the common. I decided to investigate.

I sidled in through the door, which was half open, and looked around. It was darker than Ormeley, with no carpet on the floor and smelled quite different. There were plenty of tables and chairs with people sitting on them, a high counter with stools in front of it and bottles hanging upside down on the wall behind. I padded quietly across the floor and round the side of the counter. A woman was pouring liquid from the bottles into glasses; presently she went away and came back with two steaming plates of the most heavenly looking food.

I could not help myself. I sat down and I goggled at it. I may even have drooled a little. 'Hello young fellow. After a sausage, are you?' said the woman, then she laughed. 'Eddie, here's a chap who wants your lunch.'

Eddie was sitting on a stool at the end of the bar. Now he peered round at me.

'Come on then,' he said merrily. 'Up you get.'

At first I could not believe that he was serious. At Ormeley it was strictly forbidden for animals to get up on dining-room chairs or to be fed at the table. But Eddie meant it and, after a few seconds' hesitation, I jumped up on the stool next to him. As I ate one of his sausages with all the delicacy I could manage, I little guessed that this was the beginning of a great friendship. Eddie Derbyshire and the New Inn would become permanent fixtures in my life, and we would spend many happy hours together while he put the world to rights from his bar stool.

On this day, though, I was impatient to get on with my adventure. Once my hunger was satisfied I jumped down from the stool, wagged my tail briefly at my new friends and then headed out towards Richmond Park.

I had only ever been there before with Mum. We used to walk up to the cafeteria at Pembroke Lodge, where I sometimes managed to wangle myself a sandwich when she wasn't looking. On the subject of snacks I am ashamed to admit that, on more than one occasion, I have been guilty of snatching the packed lunch of a workman taking a break in the sunshine, seated on a park bench. Clutching the paper bag in my mouth, I would then run off to the woods where the great trees, underplanted with grass and bracken, stretched away enticingly towards the horizon, and furtively guzzle my ill-gotten gains.

Here there were herds of deer. I knew better than to chase them, so it was with a certain amount of jaunty self-confidence that I set off back up Ham Gate Avenue and thence across the road towards Isabella Plantation. I had not been travelling for very long before I became aware that something was not quite right. To my left all was serene, but on my right a small herd of red deer was unsettled and beginning to move. I hurried on, eager to get out of their way, but found my path blocked. An old hind was standing, stamping her front feet, head lowered, anger in her eyes. I side-stepped, determined to avoid a confrontation. It was not my territory. Blocked again, this time by a young stag with the velvet still on his antlers. A line of them formed, shoulder to shoulder, no way forward. Back, then, that was the answer. But I was surrounded. They stood in a circle, silent, watching me.

Although deer are flight animals and, as such, a dog's natural prey, I knew enough to recognise that I was in peril. Plenty of dogs had been encircled and stamped to death by deer in the park. Mum had seen it happen.

'State your business, dog,' said the old hind.

'I ask your permission to pass through unharmed,' I said respectfully, knowing that it was essential to control my fear.

'Why? You're foe.'

'Not a friend, I know. No dog can be. But not foe. Just a traveller, asking for safe passage.'

'And what will you give us in return?'

'I can honour your customs and respect your territory. If I see your young in danger, I can warn you. If a dog chases you while I am passing through, I can come to your aid.'

Now I held the matriarch's eye with mine. I could feel her willing me to turn away. The smell of deer overwhelmed me on every side. They were getting impatient. She only had to give one signal and I would be trampled. My gaze flickered. I know she saw it because the light from her eyes became fiercer, almost unbearable. Then she said 'You may pass. But remember your pledges. We are here by Royal decree. You won't get a second chance.'

'Thank you,' I said. 'I shan't forget. My name, by the way, is Copper.'

She gave a harsh, barking cough, which I later realised was a deer's way of laughing. 'Well then, Copper. You'd better learn to be as good as gold.'

The circle parted and I was through, free again. But not just free. I knew that I had made a powerful alliance and that one day I would need to keep my part of the bargain. In the meantime it was an ideal moment to turn for home and absorb all the lessons I had learned.

The afternoon shadows were beginning to lengthen as I came to the gates of Ormeley. Jessie was at her usual lookout place on the wall. 'So you're back,' she said coolly. 'Nice time?'

'Oh yes! Wonderful. So much to tell you, Jessie.'

'Hmm. Well, you're not going to be able to do much telling if you can't get back in through the gates, are you?'

I admit I was crestfallen. I was ready for my dinner now but she was right. I had absolutely no idea how to get the gates to open for me. Jessie relented. 'You're in luck, as it happens. Mum's just about to go off in the car to fetch Jemima from a party. You'll be able to get back in then but you'd better look sharp.'

And so I did. I am afraid that Mum was not at all pleased

with me and I was sorry indeed to have caused her so much distress. I made a resolution there and then that I would never go out on my own at night and always be home in time for dinner. There was no way to tell her that I had learned how to cross a road safely or that I had formed a very unusual friendship. But, wise as she was in the ways of dogs, she knew that although the call of the wild ran strongly in my blood there was another call which would prove to be stronger still. No longer a puppy, I was a lusty young male who would soon be in search of a mate or, as it turned out, hundreds of them.

4

LOVE LIFE

Looking back on my life as an experienced old dog, I have often wondered why mating, as we call it, is so complicated for humans. All those shenanigans, all that drama associated with love and marriage, they simply do not exist for us dogs. Of course I know about love, my kind of love, the love I have for my human family: a calm kind of love.

For dogs, mating is just as important as whatever it is that humans get up to. The difference is that we make it simple. A dog smells or senses that a female needs his attention and off he goes, finds her and does the deed. Having done so, he treks off without giving her another thought because he knows there's plenty more where that came from.

I don't want to shock or, worse still, bore you with endless boasting about conquests, but I would like to tell you about the three most memorable bitches in my life: Molly, my first love; Dushka, the mother of my beloved son, the Platypus; and Doll, the most aristocratic of my mates, who shared a truly hilarious escapade with me.

I've told you a little about Molly from Manor Farm stables before. For a long time our relationship was purely playful, even rough and tumble. Then one day everything changed. She seemed different, even more beautiful, if that is possible, and unusually affectionate. As I walked home, strange smells and feelings overcame me; I found myself thinking about her. In fact, I could not stop thinking about her. Unable to get her out of my thoughts, I went back to the stables the next day. Molly flew to meet me; I felt quite overcome and mated her without really knowing what I was doing. For some reason I could not understand, we both had different reactions afterwards: Molly would not leave me alone but all I wanted to do was to go home and polish off my dinner.

The next day I had a further encounter with her, which was interrupted by a furious stablehand who chased me away with a broom. I could not help noticing, as I slunk away, that there was a queue of male dogs of all types and breeds waiting for their chance to have a go, and I was rather proud to have got there first. I did learn later that Molly was what my mother would have called 'easy' and had never been known to say no to anyone. But I like to think that she chose me as the best.

I mentioned earlier that Mum had a large litter of her own and that it divided into two. India Jane, from her first litter, lived in a cottage next door to Ormeley with her mate, Jonty, and a black dog called Dushka, whom she had rescued from a dogs' home. Dushka was not particularly beautiful but we got along all right. I did try to entice her into a bit of exploring, but she was having none of it.

'You can be as silly as you like, Copper, but India Jane says it will all end in tears if you carry on the way you are.' She was rather prim, and I couldn't resist teasing her.

One summer's day I became aware of a difference in Dushka. I had the weirdest feeling that she had become rather attractive and I kept following her around and sniffing her. This infuriated Dushka, who snapped at me and told me to get lost. But I just couldn't. I tried everything: pretend fighting, pretend play, you name it. But she just got crosser and crosser. By day three I was desperate. I had to have her, and then an idea occurred to me.

'Dushka,' I said, 'if we can nip into the kitchen, Isabel is putting down the dog bowls and you can have mine.' Dushka was very greedy.

'Very well,' she said, 'but not very clever, as the back door is shut. We can't get in.'

'Oh that's easy,' I said. 'We'll get through the cat flap. I always do.'

Dushka looked doubtful. 'It looks a bit small,' she said. And indeed it was. I hadn't been through it for months, not since I was half-grown.

'You'll be all right. On you go,' I insisted, licking my lips with anticipation.

Dushka duly put her head and front paws through the flap. There was a great deal of grunting and pushing, then, 'I'm stuck, Copper, you idiot. I can't get in and I can't get back.'

'Oh dear,' I said and quickly made my move.

Somehow my exertions managed to force Dushka through the cat flap and into the house. She was incandescent with rage. But what did I care? I had had my way, as Mum's old housekeeper, Mrs White, used to say, and there was nothing anyone could do about it. I wouldn't have minded having another go, just to make sure, but then thought better of it. Dushka was too much trouble and there were so many other willing bitches around.

And this brings me neatly to Doll. Except, of course, Doll was not her proper name, but I'll get to that in a minute. She was a white standard poodle and at first sight looked very snooty. This was partly because of the way she was clipped. Poodles, as I was shortly to learn, can be clipped in three ways: there is the pet clip, where hair is quite short all over the body; the English saddle clip, which has leg bracelets; and then there is the ghastly Continental clip, where the dog's hind end is shaved, bracelets of hair are left round the ankles and pompoms on the tail and hips. This poor girl had been given the Continental clip. But also – and this was not her fault either – standard poodles have a high, springy trot, which makes them look arrogant.

You can imagine what Mum and I thought when we used to see this apparition and her stuck-up owner mincing by. But it wasn't long before I began to suspect that an altogether different dog lurked beneath the outrageous exterior. She started to give me little sidelong glances out of the corner of her eye and it was then that I noticed how beautiful her eyes were. Very dark, they shone with a high intelligence and more than a hint of mischief. I began to hope that one day I would get to know her better. Not that I was optimistic. Mum really did not get on with her owner, Lady Smithers, so there weren't those opportunities for play and chat which came my way with other dogs.

One winter, however, the snow began to fall, and there is nothing I like more than snow. It makes me feel like a puppy all over again. I like to roll in it and chase the children's snowballs. The snow and the cold lasted for weeks and then the pond on Ham Common froze and I mean *really* froze – you could walk across it. The children became very excited and took their sledges and skates on to the common. I danced round them as they strapped on their skates and sat little Ben on to the sledge. As they skated, they pulled him along behind them across the ice and they let me hold the rope and pull him along too.

After a while I tired of this game and decided to have a wander on the common. It was a truly beautiful sight that morning: branches heavy with snow, icicles hanging from the doorways and, overhead, a bright blue sky. I watched my footprints in the snow and ran round in circles, stopping occasionally to roll over and over and over in the drifts. I must have been a comical sight when I got up, with bits of snow stuck in my eyebrows and beard and my legs looking like Ben's white socks. Suddenly I spotted the white poodle trotting ahead of me, looking like a giant snowball herself. For once she was not on a lead and her owner was nowhere in sight. I galloped up to her. She smelled wonderful.

'I'm Copper. I've seen you here often,' I began.

'I know. I've wanted to get to know you for a long time.'

'What's your name?'

She made a horrible face. 'Jolie Poupée.'

'What?'

'I know, I know. It's French for pretty doll. Awful.'

Well, I thought, you're certainly dolled up, and you *are* very pretty, whether you like it or not.

'I've got a famous hunting aunt called Dolly.' It was a lie, but I wanted to cheer her up. 'You could call yourself Doll.'

'I like it,' she said decisively. 'Much better for a gundog.'

'Gundog?' I was astounded.

'Oh yes. Standard poodles like me were always used to retrieve game from water. It's only now that we are show dogs and taken to dreadful places like Crufts.'

By now I could barely concentrate on a word she was saying. The scent of her was driving me wild. Champion. Mate. Puppies. Words at random pierced my consciousness. And then she was playing, racing round and round, tempting me, taunting, until suddenly the tone of the game changed and she became submissive.

'I love the snow, Copper,' she said, lying on her back and rolling around with her paws in the air. Despite the strong attraction I was feeling towards her, I couldn't help noticing how funny she looked with her pompoms.

'Me too. Me too,' I said, trying to manoeuvre her behind the snow-laden horse chestnut tree beside the pond. Luckily she was as keen as I was and we had a very happy time.

Doll and I were puffing and panting away, when out of

the corner of my eye I noticed Mum behaving in a very peculiar fashion. She had obviously bumped into Doll's owner, who must have been walking round the pond looking for her dog. Mum kept stepping in front of her, first one way, then the other, as Lady Smithers fidgeted, clearly anxious to walk on. But Mum simply would not get out of her way and started pointing at something behind her. I had never seen her behaving so oddly.

Then it dawned on me. She was trying to stop Lady Smithers seeing what Doll and I were up to. I had to hurry up and get the job done. Somehow I managed it, although Doll nearly gave the game away by larking around and looking very pleased with herself afterwards. I hope I am right in thinking that she'd had the time of her life. She certainly looked as if she had.

Later, walking back with Mum, Mimi and the children, I listened to them talking about what had happened. I was right; Mum had seen Doll and me mating and had frantically tried to prevent Lady Smithers seeing it too. Doll was about to be sent off to a very expensive stud dog, a former Crufts winner, and Lady Smithers was banking on some champion puppies.

'Worth hundreds of pounds each, apparently,' said Mum.

'Not now, they won't be,' replied Mimi in her dourest northern voice. She didn't like snobs. 'They will be little Coppers, just like my friend here, and all the better for it.'

I smirked, and Mum and Mimi laughed all the way back to Ormeley.

5

THE DOG SHOW

I had said to Bungle that I was going to take his advice and find my family, but I didn't really have any idea where to start. It seemed important to retrace my steps to the place where I was born but I did not know in which direction that lay. I knew that once on the road I had strength, endurance and enough common sense to negotiate most hazards. The deer had given me leave to roam Richmond Park unmolested and I was confident that I could safely cross roads on my own. I could beg or steal food on the way. But how to identify my destination, or indeed precisely what to do when I got there? These things were hazy in my mind. I decided to talk to my old mentors Tessa and Flora.

I could tell at once that I had worried them. Neither of them said anything for several minutes. Then Flora began. 'Look here, Copper. What exactly are you after?'

'To find my mother – if she's still alive, that is.'

'It's a bad idea. You've been spending too much time with human families.'

'I don't care,' I said stubbornly. 'I want to find my mother.'

Tessa nudged me gently. 'Sit down,' she said. 'There are obviously one or two things you don't know about bitches and their puppies. Had your mother begun to send you away before she disappeared?'

'What do you mean?' My heart was suddenly full of fear.

'I mean that all good mothers, after the first few weeks, teach their puppies about dominance and submission. If a pup doesn't learn that, then he won't survive in a pack – or with human beings, for that matter.'

Flora took up the story, explaining that when we were four to five weeks old, our mother should have started to nip us when we tried to suckle, she should have walked away at times when we wanted to snuggle up to her, until finally we were quite independent and able not only to fend for ourselves but also to be obedient to pack hierarchy.

'I suppose,' I said, dredging my memory, 'I suppose she *had* started a bit of nipping and scolding. But not much. Does it matter?'

'It certainly does. And if you find her, we think you're going to be disappointed. She probably won't recognise you.'

'Well, I wouldn't expect her to right away. I'm a grown dog now.'

'No, I mean that bitches don't know or care about their pups once they are separated from them. And normally pups don't care about their mothers. It's nature, you see. But *animal* nature, not human nature, not like Mum is with her children.'

'To hell with nature,' I said, 'I'm going to look for her.'

'Oh well,' Tessa's eyes were worried but her voice was kind, 'we'd better discuss how you are to find your way back to where you were born.' And then she began to speak about the great secrets of animal travel; of how flocks of birds can find their way across thousands of miles of uncharted land and sea; of huge fish that swim from the river to the ocean and then back to the place of their birth to spawn. And she spoke about the ancient drovers' roads, where men and their dogs drove herds of cattle from the Scottish Highlands to England, from Wales to London, and then set the dogs free to find their own way home.

'They feel the pull, you see,' said Flora.

'The pull? Like a tug of war?'

'No. The magnetic pull. You haven't been to the sea yet but when you do, you'll notice how the tide goes in and out. In fact, you'll see it near here with the river. Sometimes the water is high, lapping against the banks. Sometimes it is low, just a narrow channel and you could walk out on to the mud flats. The moon pulls the sea tide in and out, and the sea pulls the river. In the same way, magnetic paths under our feet cross and criss-cross the earth, drawing us home, pointing the way.

'You'll need to learn how to read these rhythms and feel

the magnetic pulse of the earth.' She stopped for a moment, apparently lost in thought. Then she went on. 'The clues are everywhere. You must listen to the wind. Watch the sun, the moon and the stars. Your path will find you and then, I promise, no human road can distract you from your destination. You will be homeward bound.'

A shiver of excitement ran through me at Flora's words. I could not wait to begin. Win, lose or draw, I would seek my luck on the secret pathways of our world. If I found my mother, so much the better. But lay her ghost to rest, by finding the place of my birth, that I could and would do.

'But Copper,' it was Tessa, 'Copper, my dear, we really do advise leaving it until after the dog show.'

'Dog show? What dog show?' Memories of darling Doll danced in my mind. Weren't dog shows her idea of hell?

'The dog show that Mum is organising at Ormeley very soon.'

I was astonished. I knew about Crufts, of course, and I thought Mum despised it as much as I did.

I had first become aware of Crufts when I was lying on Mum's bed watching television. Drifting in and out of sleep, eyes half-closed, I suddenly noticed a lot of dogs parading up and down in a ring. All of them were on leads, either being walked or being made to run by their owners and then stopping in front of another man, who seemed to run his hands all over them. I could not believe my eyes; there were all sorts, from big tall hunting dogs to toy dogs, tiny little things. I quickly became engrossed. I could see that Mum was biting her nails and I could tell by her exclamations that she was praying the border collie or the Irish setter would win and hoping that it would not be the shitzu or the Pekinese. She became quite voluble on the subject. 'No, no, not that one, you blind fool! Look at the one on the left! Oh you idiot, I don't believe it!'

As the judge beckoned with his hand and a small furry dog was hauled in, he totally ignored the beautiful saluki at the end of the row. I was indignant too, but for a different reason. How could any dog take part in a thing like that? How undignified to run around a ring at the end of a lead and allow yourself to be felt all over. I would not have been able to resist giving the judge's hand a sharp bite.

And they were planning one of these abominations at Ormeley!

I need hardly tell you that it was see-all, hear-all Jessie who filled me in on all the details. 'Mum may not like dog shows,' she said, 'but this one is different. This is being given for charity. It's for Blue Cross, the hospital that looks after dogs and cats. If the owners are poor they don't even have to pay. The hospital only exists because of people like Mum, who raise money for it. You see,' she went on, licking her paws, 'I know all about it because my mother had her kittens there, including me. There were four of us and that's why I'm here. Mum found me at Blue Cross. Mind you, I'm going to keep well clear and out of the way on the day. You and I get on quite well but most dogs like to chase cats and I don't intend to be the titbit they are rewarded with at the end of it all.'

I felt somewhat bewildered by all this information, but

soon it seemed that everyone, both inside and outside Ormeley, was talking of nothing else. On Ham Common, Bungle bustled up to me and said that he was getting clipped specially for the day. My lovely Afghan friend Honey, who had once knelt down on a memorable day in the park to make it easier for me to mate with her, was going to be shampooed and combed until her beautiful blonde fur was as soft and silky as a cat's. Jenny, a spaniel bitch whom I had also loved, was practising retrieving sticks as though her life depended on it.

At first, quite frankly, I felt that this was all a bit beneath me but, then, as I realised that no one seemed to be preparing me for any special appearance, or grooming my coat until it shone, I began to get a bit upset. Not only that, the household itself seemed to have gone mad. Mimi, Mum, Maria, Isabel and Arnaldo thought and talked about nothing but the blessed dog show: what the judges were going to have for lunch, how big the tent should be, where it would go, how many classes to have and how many chairs would be needed for spectators.

Now, I am about as independent as a dog can be and even my worst enemy would not accuse me of being a wimp, but no dog – and I mean really *no* dog – can bear his household being turned upside down. You might think that because I led a very free life, getting in and out of Ormeley whenever I wanted, that I wouldn't care about the house being in an uproar. But I did care, very much.

As the paddock was roped off and the tent arrived, I felt more and more annoyed. After all, it was my garden and it was up to me to choose which dogs were welcome there and which were not. I don't want you to think that I sulked or that I didn't try to rise above it and take an interest. I did. But I tell you, the most sainted dog on earth would have had his patience tested that day.

The show was scheduled to take place on a Sunday. Some of the participants and most of the judges had been invited to a buffet lunch in the house before the show, which was due to start at two o'clock in the afternoon. Most of the dogs taking part were left in the cars while their owners ate lunch in the dining room. There were four judges: the writer Jilly Cooper; Mr Millington, a famous dog-breeder; Lord Oaksey, a horse-racing expert; and a very important and well-known lady called Barbara Woodhouse, who had written a book called *No Bad Dogs*. Hmmm, I thought, we'll see.

By far the nicest of the judges was Jilly. She had brought her two dogs, Barbara and Mabel, who were a bit shy to start with but soon let me know that they fancied me. I began to feel a bit better and then cheered up a lot when I realised that Jilly was quite taken with me and with Jemima. Perhaps this was going to be more fun than I had thought.

After lunch we all trooped out into the garden and over to the paddock, which by now was filled with dogs and owners. There, to my fury, I was put on a lead by Mum. Looking at the array of contestants, I could see two small black spaniels, including Jenny, several labradors and a flat-coated retriever called Louis, whom I knew, as he was one of India Jane's dogs. There were also a couple of King Charles spaniels and a Pekinese or two, with their squashed faces, among the others.

Each of the judges had a class to themselves and Barbara Woodhouse was overseeing them all. She sat in a wheelchair and spoke very loudly and clearly in the kind of tone I would not like to have disobeyed. Jemima had begged Mum to enter me in every single one of the classes but Mum had refused, so there I was, the host dog, on a lead and not even allowed to show myself off. I sat quietly but I was furious. I would give them all the slip and join the other dogs, if it was the last thing I did.

My chance came during the obedience class. As the dogs trotted around the ring, Mum was called away and Jemima, accidentally on purpose, let go of my lead. Without a moment's hesitation I rushed in. I must say that all the dogs were very friendly and I made sure they knew I was the real host of the show. As they were sitting or walking to command, I decided the time had come to liven things up. I tore wildly around the ring and playfully mounted Louis, not in a mating sort of way, just wrestling.

'Come on, Louis,' I panted, 'let's go and chase some squirrels by the bird table.'

'I can't, Copper,' said Louis, moving sedately round the ring with his owner, trying in vain to shake me off his back. 'I have to be obedient and then I might win a rosette.'

'A rosette? What's that?' I said, trying to roll him over in a wrestling hold.

'Get off, Copper!' said Louis crossly. 'We have to take this seriously. Quick, the judge is looking at me.'

As he spoke, a booming voice echoed across the garden. 'Would someone kindly remove that brown mongrel from the ring.' It was Barbara Woodhouse.

Mum wasn't in sight and Jemima was giggling, so I continued my display of high jinks: tearing round the ring and trying to entice Jenny, the black spaniel, into a chase.

'No, Copper, no,' she said, trying to look demure. 'I am odds-on to win this class because I've had training.'

'Training!' I yelled, quite over the top by now. 'I'll show you training,' and I grabbed her lead and tried to pull her out of the ring.

Again the voice boomed. 'Would someone please remove that dog immediately. Its behaviour is disgraceful. If it can't be controlled it should be shut in the house until the show is over.'

At that moment, Mum appeared. 'Copper,' she shouted angrily, 'come here at once, you naughty boy!'

It was too late. I was now beside myself with excitement and the desire to show off to those lead-held dogs. I raced on to the main lawn adjacent to the paddock, running round and round, hoping they were watching me and envying my freedom as I tossed my rubber bone into the air. Then, to show Mrs Woodhouse exactly what I thought of her, I squatted down in the middle of the lawn and – well, I'll leave it to your imagination. There isn't really a polite word for it that I can think of. But if I tell you that you wouldn't want to step in it, you'll know what I mean. As Mum, red-faced, ran after me, I pranced back into the show ring to demonstrate again to the other dogs what a lad I was.

Then I heard a gentle voice say, 'Come on, Copper, your mum is getting really upset.' It was Jilly. She picked up my lead and gave it to Mum, who was furious.

'Don't be cross,' said Jilly. 'He's so adorable and it's understandable that he feels left out with all this happening on his territory.'

Meekly, I allowed myself to be led away and for the rest of the show I sat in the tent and watched all the pedigree dogs perform. I think the overall winner was a King Charles spaniel, who walked round the ring with a very conceited look on his face. I saw that my friends Louis and Jenny had won something, as they were wearing those rosettes I had so mocked. In my heart of hearts I really wished I had one too, pinned to my collar.

The King Charles spaniel's owner was given a silver cup, and as he was graciously receiving it I felt someone putting something on my collar. It was a bright red rosette and I heard a little voice say, 'You would have been my choice, Copper, in the best of breed.' It was Jemima, filled with indignation that I had not won every class. Jilly's dogs won the class for the dog who looks most like its owner. Although I was pleased for them, I could not, for the life of me, see the likeness.

6

THE SEARCH

I had fallen into the habit of leaving Ormeley every day, for by now everyone accepted that I was allowed to come and go quite freely on the understanding that I was home by nightfall. Sometimes I went for a few hours, wandering here and there, sometimes from breakfast till dinner time. Some mornings I would wander down to Manor Farm and romp with Molly. It was an easy trot along the pavements once I had crossed over the road at the Ham Common lights. One day I was discussing my plans with her when she said 'The river. Copper, you've got to get along to the river. For a start, there are boats of all sorts that travel up and down, many of them with dogs on board who may know things, and secondly you can go for miles undisturbed along the towpath.'

I felt that this was good advice for, as yet, I had not encountered the magnetic pull which the collies had talked about. I had tried to ask the ducks and the seagulls on Ham Common how they navigated their flights but I suppose I should have realised they wouldn't talk to me. After my first escapade there I had become known as an ignorant cur and no amount of humility on my part would persuade them that my duck-chasing days were over. Quacking, hissing, wing-flapping contempt met every overture I made.

Bungle, as you can imagine, was no help either. He thought the collies were a bit mad, and that talk of magnetic paths was mere moonshine. 'Shaggy-dog stories, my dear Copper. Wouldn't give them the time of day, myself.'

Oddly enough, the greatest encouragement of my dream came from the most unexpected quarter. Jessie – cool, cynical, self-centred Jessie – said out of the blue one evening 'You know what? Your problem is that you're all over the place.' Oh here we go, I thought.

'The collies told you what to do,' she reminded me. 'They said, watch, listen, feel for the magnetic pull. You're bustling about like Bungle. All bark and no bite. Settle down, be still. And when the time comes, I'll help you.'

I was speechless. Jessie, who had given me nothing but grief when I wanted to leave Ormeley. Jessie, who had greeted my first thwarted escape with condescending sarcasm. What on earth had come over her? And then she went on, 'We can find the way back to where you were born. I'm sure of it. That isn't the problem. The problem is what we're going to do when we get there.'

'Ask around?'

'Oh yes? And who exactly are you going to ask?'

'That's easy. There were loads of cats who lived there. I could ask the foxes too but they'll only come out at night and I've always promised I'd be home for dinner so as not to worry Mum.'

'And you think the cats will talk to you?'

I hesitated, a bit uncertain. 'You don't think they will?'

'I am one hundred per cent sure they won't. Your mother hated them. She taught you to despise them. The last thing they'll want to do is help you to find her.' She thought for a moment, methodically washing her face with one paw, the end of her black tail lightly twitching. Then she said, 'You're going to have to leave this one with me. They're not going to like me much either, but at least I talk their language. I'll play it by ear.'

'Can we go tomorrow, Jessie?'

But she was hardly listening. In the last half-hour the moon had risen, bright in the sky outside, and her eyes had got bigger and bigger until now they were huge lamps of green fire. Jessie the predator was ready for a night's hunting. I was about to lose her.

'Jessie, please, I know you've got to go but tell me, when can we set out? I won't sleep a wink till I know.'

'Moon's got to be right. I'll tell you when.'

'But,' I began stupidly, 'but we can't go at night.'

'Great cats of Egypt!' Jessie spat contemptuously. 'Don't you know *anything*?'

And then she was gone, streaking through the cat flap as

though the hounds of hell were on her tail. I am not a patient dog but at that moment I needed all the patience I could muster. Once Jessie had been hunting she would sleep the whole of the following day, so our expedition certainly would not be tomorrow.

Instead I decided to check out the river as Molly had advised, and on my way I would stop off at the Dysart Arms. Like the New Inn on Ham Common, this pub had become one of my favourite haunts. It was set slightly back from the road and it was quite easy to slip in through a door into the bar, once you knew your way. Inside, it was dark and cosy and smelled of beer and smoke. I often thought that once the doors of the Dysart Arms shut on those regulars who came every day, the outside world ceased to exist.

One of those who lunched there every day was a wrinkled old fellow called Bob. Bob liked to smoke, he liked to drink and he liked to talk. On this particular day he said something that interested me a lot. Bob, like Eddie at the New Inn, had rather taken me under his wing; he, too, used to let me get up on a bar stool and often shared his lunch with me. Today was no exception: 'Hello, old fellow. Come to see me, have you? Up you get.' Then, turning to Trevor the barman: 'This chap reminds me of a dog I knew in the war. Same deep old eyes. Name of Scooter.'

'Oh yeah?'

'Yes. Now this dog was extraordinary. He could foretell air raids.'

'You don't say.'

'Not a word of a lie. And we never ever found out how

he did it. I wouldn't like to guess the number of lives that dog saved. About ten minutes before the sirens sounded, Scooter would be barking at the back door to go out. He was never wrong.'

I wonder if I could have done that, I thought. I bet I could. Then I pricked up my ears again as Bob, Trevor and a third man at the bar fell into a lengthy discussion about animal telepathy and about dogs and cats who had travelled for miles across strange territory to find lost owners. So Flora and Tessa aren't the silly old fools that Bungle says they are, I thought, as I slipped down from my stool and headed back towards River Lane. And Jessie was spot on, as well.

River Lane is a very narrow road that curves down from the main road towards the Thames. On the left, on the corner of the lane, was a house that sat back from the road, with high gates and a wall. There was a brass sign on the gates that always made Mum laugh. It said: 'Beware of the dog. Enter at your own risk.' She said we ought to have one at Ormeley. But the odd thing was that I never heard or saw a sign of a dog there at all. It made me mighty curious, I can tell you.

I trotted down between the houses until the lane opened up, with fields on the right hand side. There were always cows there. I would have liked to have scampered about a bit in those fields but Tessa and Flora had given me a healthy respect for cows. 'They hate us,' they'd said. 'Much more than they hate sheep, who are just dim and ignorant. If you think your encounter with the deer was frightening, just you try getting the wrong side of a herd of cattle.'

As I passed by, some were lying down but others were watching me, staring and blowing clouds of steam, jostling and pushing up against the fence.

'That's the other thing about cattle. Nothing can hold them in once they are stampeding. You don't want to rely on a fence to save you,' the collies had said.

I lowered my head respectfully and avoided eye contact. The last thing I wanted was any trouble and I knew that a dog on the move was like a red rag to a bull – so to speak.

Finally, I reached the river.

Perhaps it was the stories that Tessa and Flora had told me, but the most terrific surge of excitement rushed through me at the sight of that mighty stretch of water. A light breeze had got up while I was in the pub and it was ruffling the surface, making the sunlight dance and play on the ripples. I lifted my nose and sniffed the air; the mixture of smells was unbelievably heady. I seemed to be able to catch the bright, salty scent of the sea – or at least what I took to be the sea – with its promise of far-off adventures, and yet underlying it was something old, stale, deliciously rotten, like the garbage of which I sometimes caught whiffs as I passed garden gates. I daresay this particular smell might not excite a human being, but to a dog it was pure heaven: a bit fishy, a bit muddy, mixed with some old vegetation and other things that you probably wouldn't want to hear about.

As I was standing there, lost in a delightful reverie, I heard a sharp yapping and realised that a boat was moored a few yards down-river. Standing in the back, furiously wagging its short, stumpy tail, was a small, jaunty-looking dog with a brown and white splodgy coat with one ear up and one ear down.

'Ahoy there,' he yipped. 'What's your business?'

'Just looking,' I said. 'What's your name?'

'Oh, I'm Toby,' he replied cheerfully. 'I'm minding the boat while the boss is shopping. Want to come aboard and have a look around?'

And so I did. Toby was a Jack Russell terrier and his boss was a man given to mad enthusiasms. One minute he was spending every day on his allotment, trying to grow enormous vegetables, the next he was gripped by sea fever, convinced that he should live the rest of his life on a boat. This was the boating phase and Toby said it was definitely preferable to the allotment. 'Though I'm not really built for the water,' he confided. 'My family were bred to kill rats and to go to ground to bolt foxes. I see those damned rats swimming about all the time but I'm not the fastest swimmer and they're devils to catch hold of when they're wet.'

The sun was warm on our backs, the boat was rocking gently and Toby and I were on such cordial terms that presently we settled down in the bows to snooze and chat amiably about this and that. He told me about mighty struggles underground between his father – a hunt terrier – and a fox with half a tail, which was often hunted but never caught.

'The word was that he lived in a tree, but one day they ran

him to earth and sent my father in after him. You couldn't have found a better fighter than my father but even he was no match for the bob-tailed fox. Lost an eye in that scrap and was never as brave again.'

Then there was Toby's sister, who went to ground after rabbits and was lost for three whole weeks. 'She was found in the nick of time by a dowser. They swing crystals over maps until they get a special signal.'

'I wish one of them would find the place where I was born,' I said wistfully. And then the whole story tumbled out.

When I got to the end, Toby said thoughtfully, 'The business about the moon. The thing your cat said. It reminds me of this boss of mine when he was growing vegetables. He used to say you had to sow at the waxing of the moon and harvest at the waning. If it's anything to do with that, then Jessie'll be waiting for the new moon.'

I was about to say that I couldn't see what on earth growing vegetables had to do with finding my mother, when Toby's head went up, his ears pricked. 'Quick, Copper. Better scarper. Boss's back. Been nice meeting you. Hope I see you around. And good luck with everything.'

In a flash he was on his feet, tail going, and I made a bound for the towpath. Time to go home for dinner and see what mood Jessie was in.

She was sitting on the windowsill, quite still, looking just like a china cat. I didn't really enjoy talking to her at that angle, as it made me feel at a disadvantage, but at least she was not asleep.

'Jessie, Jessie. When's the new moon?'

She glanced down at me, green eyes inscrutable, whiskers tucked back. Then she yawned, showing her rough pink tongue and every one of her sharp teeth. The angle of her whiskers changed very slightly. I could have sworn she was smiling. 'You're learning, Copper. We go a week on Monday.'

I decided that I would try not to waste a moment between now and the date Jessie had set for our departure. If I could get a sense – any sense at all – of the direction in which we should travel, then our task would be so much easier.

And so I wandered the park and the common, I visited the Dysart Arms a couple of times and shared a sausage or two with Bob, and I trotted up and down the towpath beside the river. Once I was hailed by Toby, cheery as ever on his boat, but, try as I might, I could get no sense of pull in any specific direction.

Then one morning, as I was standing at the Ham Common lights, waiting to cross, I felt something – very slight at first, but then more insistent. It was a sense, an instinct, a kind of tugging, nagging feeling, no more precise than that, telling me to turn away from my usual path and look left instead of right. A bus was stopping just beyond the lights. I nipped along the pavement and hopped on board. I knew perfectly well that I was likely to be thrown off once the conductor realised I was travelling alone, but I managed five stops before that happened. It was enough, for the further we went the stronger my sense of direction grew.

Something, someone, was pulling me. Whether it was my birthplace, the butcher's shop, the distant scent of a bitch on heat, or something as yet unknown, I could not tell. But it was there.

Meanwhile the old moon waned day by day, just as Jessie had foretold, and the new moon rose, a clear, pale sliver of light in the sky, a beacon for our journey.

'Tomorrow, Copper, first thing. Mind you're ready on time.'

As if I wouldn't be!

The day dawned still and quite bright. As Jessie and I slipped out through the gates, she said, 'Look, Copper, up there.' And I saw, bone-white against the greyish blue of the sky, the faint but unmistakable outline of the new moon again.

We followed exactly the path I had taken a few days earlier. Right out of Ormeley gates, down Ham Gate Avenue, left into Upper Ham Road. Then on to the bus towards Kingston, until we were spotted and thrown off. Now we settled into a purposeful rhythm, careful not to get in the way of pedestrians, wary of making eye contact with anyone, animal or human, who we might meet walking towards us. I don't mean by this that we didn't see things. While appearing to be oblivious of our surroundings, deaf and blind to the people and traffic surging around us, we in fact noticed and stored away endless details of our route and of milestones along the way.

We saw plenty of dogs and cats as we travelled. A boy

dressed in filthy clothes, sitting on a sleeping bag on the pavement, held out a hat for money while his dog – probably a labrador-collie cross – sat patiently by his side. Not the life I should have liked, I thought. Then there was an Alsatian, rattling in fury up and down on the end of a chain while we took a short cut through a builder's yard. How glad we were to see him tied up! And two Shetland sheepdogs were tethered outside a supermarket, watching over a baby in a pram. They wagged their plumed tails gently to and fro on the ground when I said, 'No harm, friends. We're just travellers.'

We saw cats on cars and under cars, sleeping on dustbin lids, perched on windowsills and even prowling on rooftops. As we passed through one of the back streets with little square houses standing side by side, we saw two vast women, with arms like hams, leaning on their garden gates. On the wall between them, sunning himself sleepily, was a ginger cat so large that he seemed to billow out on each side.

''E gets everything 'e wants,' remarked one of the giantesses contentedly to the other as we came within earshot.

'And it'll be the death of him, by the look of things,' muttered Jessie. But the ginger cat turned out to have a good sense of humour because he opened one big amber eye and winked at us.

All the time as we travelled, I could feel something taking us onwards. Every now and again I worried: 'I suppose we do know where we are going, do we, Jessie?'

'Keep going, don't think,' she replied tersely.

At length the pulse, the pull, the feeling, or whatever you wanted to call it, became stronger and stronger, until it was almost painful. We had been trotting along a main road for some time. On one side were shabby, deserted shops, on the other, desolate stretches of wasteland, some enclosed by high mesh fences, some not. It was on one of these roads that I suddenly felt absolutely certain we had arrived.

We turned aside and began to pick our way across rough grass, treading gingerly to avoid the broken glass and cans that littered the ground at intervals. The smell of tomcat was everywhere, rank and sour. Sometimes I caught a whiff of fox. Then we came to what seemed to be an enclosure, bounded by a tumbledown wall. Behind that more grass, weeds, nettles, tyres, old coils of wire – and a sudden scuttling blur of movement as about five or six small animals scattered in front of us.

'Wild kittens,' hissed Jessie. 'Watch out now.'

And in a moment we were surrounded. Cats – what seemed to be dozens of them – growling, spitting, warning us to be on our way, unless we wanted our eyes scratched out.

'We mean no disrespect,' said Jessie. I had never heard her so humble. 'We're looking for news of Copper's mother.' As she spoke, she fluffed herself up to twice her normal size. This was a trick of Jessie's that I envied tremendously. While she kept her voice low and polite, she looked quite menacing. 'She left a litter of puppies here one day and never came back.'

'Good riddance. Hope they starved.' The voice came from a lean tabby cat with a patchy, staring coat and ribs which you could count one by one. I bristled and my hackles rose.

'Steady Copper,' warned Jessie, who then addressed the cats, 'You may have heard or seen something. She was quite well-known in these parts.'

'There's a bitch with a litter in the shed over there. Now get off our land and don't come back.'

My heart was thudding against my ribs as we picked our way towards the shed. Was this where I was born? Was it possible that my mother had survived and come back to whelp here again?

The shed was very dark inside and at first we could see nothing. Then from a corner at the back came a low, rumbling growl and the flicking movement of what could have been a tail. We moved forward cautiously.

Out of the dark, a thunderbolt of bone and fur and muscle launched itself at me, rolling me over and over in the dirt, then a heavy body pinned me down. I felt hot breath, teeth at my throat. We had ended up near the door; as the light filtered over us, I looked up into the face of a bitch ready to deliver the killing bite and the eyes that stared back at me were my own.

How long we looked at each other I do not know, but in the end I had no option but to turn my gaze away and bare my undefended throat to her. I lay quite still and made my body go soft and floppy. Gradually I felt her relax in return and at last she stepped over me and let me get to my feet. I stood, with my head and tail lowered and my eyes averted, waiting for permission to speak.

'Well then,' she demanded, 'what's all this about? I've got eight pups in here to feed.'

'I was looking for the place where I was born. I think it might have been here. I had nine brothers and sisters. We were left alone when our mother disappeared. One of the bitch pups died.'

There was such a long silence that I dared to peep sideways at her. She was staring intently, not at me but into the distance. Again I had the strangest sensation that I was looking at myself. At length she said, 'Did you end up in a butcher's shop?'

My heart began to thud again. Not my mother, then, but a sister?

'Yes.'

'You were the first to go. I was next, but my owner died and I ended up on the street. It isn't so bad once you get used to it.'

'Have you seen our mother again?'

'No.' Her voice was sharp. 'And I wouldn't want to any more than this lot will want to see me again once they're launched on the world. It isn't our way.'

At that moment I felt a huge sense of sadness and relief all mixed into one. Sadness that I had lost my mother too young, relief that I had landed on my feet with my human family, sadness that my sister was living rough, relief that she was there at all. Now I could go home.

'Goodbye and good luck,' I said. But I am not sure that my sister even heard me. She had already turned away to reassure her puppies.

On the way back, Jessie, who had discreetly retired to the top of an old oil drum until it was safe to come out, said, 'Now then, Copper, are we done with all that?'

'Yes, Jessie.'

'Good, because you've got a job to do. The Platypus needs you.'

7

THE PLATYPUS

Of all the hundreds of pups that I am proud to say I sired, the Platypus was by far the most beloved. After the cat-flap episode, Dushka had produced two puppies by me and Mum had decided to keep one. He was the oddest-looking thing you have ever seen. Black from head to toe like his mother, he had a broad forehead like a labrador, a rather pointed nose, a long sleek body and short, comical little legs. I loved him on sight.

Mum called him the Platypus because someone had said that he resembled a creature called the duck-billed platypus. She looked it up in an animal book and laughingly showed everyone a photograph. Personally I could never see the likeness but if it made Mum happy, well then, I was happy too. I loved to hear her laugh. Mum liked a joke and the smallest things would set her off. Perhaps this was the luckiest of all the lucky things that happened to me in my life. An owner with no sense of humour would not have understood me or given me the freedom that Mum did. I hope she knows how grateful I am to her.

By now I was an experienced traveller. I had learned a good trick for crossing roads after watching how a very old, lame Alsatian brought the traffic to a standstill, long after the lights had changed. Following his example, I would hold one paw up and hobble off the kerb on three legs. Cars would always stop to let me cross the road. Once on the other side, away I went on four legs again. A friend of Mum's caught me doing it and told her. I don't think she could quite believe at first that an animal could work out such a thing. Of course, Mum found it highly amusing. She might have found it less funny if she had known that now I planned to teach the Platypus everything I knew.

He fitted in quite easily to the Ormeley routine and everyone liked him. Flora and Tessa still stayed outside in their kennel but would always come with us for walks in Richmond Park, especially when Jimmy was home. I was never quite sure in those days what I thought about Jimmy or, for that matter, what he thought about me. I suppose I found it hard to accept a top dog who was away so much, and, in addition to that, I had begun to realise that if Mum ever seemed a bit depressed, it usually had something to do with her missing him. I don't like the people I love being unhappy – no dog does – and I always did my very best to cheer her up, usually by bringing her a present like a sock or a shoe. Luckily, as I've said, it was easy to make Mum laugh.

The Platypus made *everyone* laugh. In fact it seemed almost impossible for a human being to look at him without giggling. After a while I got rather shirty about this. Robin, Mum's second son, annoyed me particularly when he said, 'Come on, that's not one of Copper's sons. I bet a dachshund got to Dushka first.'

Look at his sweet nature, I wanted to shout. See his charm. I'd know my own son anywhere.

'All right, all right,' I admitted irritably to Jessie afterwards, 'his physique is not quite what I'd have expected from my bloodlines, but look at his eyes. All my children inherit the eyes.'

'Does it really matter?' she said calmly. 'He thinks he's your son. You feel you're his father. I'd forget about the rest if I were you.'

She was right. The Platypus was playful, loving and amiable. He wanted to do everything that I did: drink from the same bowl, eat from the same dish and sleep in the same basket. Gradually I stopped sticking so close to Mum, and the Platypus and I slept curled around each other every night. I suppose it was inevitable that as he grew up he would want to go adventuring with me. In fact it was the last thing I really wanted, but soon it became apparent that either I would have to learn to stay indoors or the Platypus would have to learn how to travel with me. In life, we imagine that there are endless choices requiring us to make decisions. But when it comes right down to it, there is generally only one path left open to us in any situation. And so it was here. The Platypus would have to learn how to travel.

'I'm going to teach you quite a few tricks that other domestic dogs don't know,' I said to him. 'But you've got to make me a solemn promise before I do.'

'Yes. Oh yes!' he said eagerly.

'You must promise me, with Jessie as our witness, that you will never try any of them on your own. You and I go together – or we don't go at all.'

'I promise. I promise!'

'Jessie?'

'Yes, Copper, I heard. Just mind you stick to it, little Platypus.'

'Oh yes, I will.'

And we knew he would. He may have been my son but he had not inherited my fierce, rebellious streak. Like most things in canine and human affairs, it would prove to be both his strength and his weakness.

I started with the easiest but most important lesson: how to travel safely for miles down roads.

'Don't,' I told him, 'don't embark on a route unless you can see a pavement or a grass verge stretching away in front of you. You may think it is safe enough to sneak along down the side of the road itself, but it isn't. You can get knocked off your feet by a car or cycle coming too close to you, get drenched in water, cut your paws on glass or get swept under the wheels of a lorry. We all have to cross roads, and I've taught you how to do that, but otherwise roads are for cars, lorries and bikes, not for dogs.'

Then I explained that if we wanted to travel for a long

way successfully on our own, we must learn to be invisible. That meant being as unobtrusive yet as quietly purposeful as possible. Above all, he must not make eye contact with other dogs or people.

'I mean it, Platypus. I won't take you if you're going to try to make friends with everyone on the way. We won't make it past Ham Common.'

The Platypus looked sheepish. He was terribly inquisitive and found it almost impossible not to strike up a conversation with anyone he met. 'What, not be friendly to *anyone*?'

I sighed because I knew I also had to teach him about the long stare.

'Every now and again you will meet a dog who wants an argument or even just to get in your way. In those cases you need to use your eye to stare him down. Let's have a go and see how you get on. Look me in the eye. Stare through me, far away, as if through the back of my head.'

Poor darling Platypus. He just could not get the hang of it. His eyes flickered, he blinked, he wagged his tail apologetically. Finally he gave an enormous yawn and turned his head aside.

'Oh Platypus.'

'Sorry, Copper.'

'Never mind. We'll just have to keep you out of trouble.'

There was no avoiding it. The Platypus was not a dog who had inherited the long stare from my bloodline. I minded about that in a son of mine, but there was nothing I could do about it.

'It's born, not made, you know,' remarked Tessa on one of our walks.

'Yes,' I said glumly, 'I can see that.'

At first the Platypus and I just made local excursions. On Ham Common, we met Bungle. 'I'm surprised he doesn't look more like you, Copper,' he said tactlessly. 'Are you sure he's yours?'

'Quite sure,' I said shortly.

'Ah. Funny, but I can't remember Dushka having a good word to say about you. And of course she did get around a fair bit.'

There are times when friendship gets tested to its limits and this was one of them. 'Bungle,' I said, my hackles on end, my legs and tail stiff with fury, 'Bungle, if you say another word, I shall tear your head off.'

'No need for that kind of talk, old friend,' said Bungle hastily. 'No offence meant.'

'Good,' I said. 'Come on, Platypus. We're going to the pub.'

At the New Inn, I introduced him to Eddie who, as usual, greeted me like an old friend. 'Who's this, then? Come to stand us a round?'

We wagged our tails and were rewarded with a piece of chicken each. Then it was on to the Dysart Arms, to Bob and a sausage apiece. Finally it was time to show the Platypus the river and to see if we could locate Toby.

We were in luck. There was the boat, bobbing beside the towpath, with Toby on guard. I looked doubtfully at the

Platypus's little legs and knew that he would never make it on to the boat.

'Care for a stroll down the path?' I called out.

In a second Toby was by our side, tail and body wagging and wriggling with pleasure. Introductions done, he sniffed the Platypus all over and said appreciatively 'You're just built to go to ground. Ever thought of it? You could be very useful against badgers. Not,' he added quickly, 'that it's quite the done thing these days.'

At the word badgers, I stiffened. I knew perfectly well that dachshunds were once used to go to ground after them in Germany. The dachshunds on the common were always boasting about it.

'Toby,' I growled.

But Toby pressed on as if I hadn't spoken. 'What a look of you he's got, Copper.'

My anger evaporated. I couldn't help a pleased smirk.

'It's the eyes,' he went on. 'I'd know them anywhere.'

Perhaps he only said it to be kind. For all his cocky, jaunty ways, Toby was a surprisingly sensitive dog. But I chose to believe that it was just as he said. The Platypus had my eyes because he was my son.

It was time to become more adventurous, time to explore the secret paths and wild corners of Richmond Park; time to teach him about the deer and to make sure that he understood about the pact I had made with them. I decided on a trip to the Albert, a favourite pub of mine at Kingston Gate.

On the way back, I noticed two lurchers on the loose in the park. Now, the thing about long dogs and lurchers is this:

indoors they are the most peaceful, cosy animals imaginable, a bit like Jessie. But also like Jessie, once out of doors, they are born killers. Just let something – anything – get up in front of them and they have to chase it. But not only chase it: they have to chase to kill and kill to eat. As I watched them, out of the corner of my eye I saw what seemed to be a large hare emerge from the bracken. Except it wasn't a hare: it was a baby red deer, bewildered, looking for its mother.

'Back, go back!' I barked.

The baby froze; up went the lurchers' heads. Then, swift as arrows, they were gone. It can only have been seconds before they had their prey. I am a dog who likes chasing and killing squirrels as much as anyone. But this was different. The cries of her dying child brought the hind to the scene. Frantically she circled and stamped then stood there, indecisive. And I knew that she, too, would die unless she ran before the lurchers saw her. She would only run if chased.

'Come on, Platypus,' I said urgently. I ran as I had never run before. When I reached her I went for her heels, barking furiously. Avoiding her whirling feet with their deadly sharp hooves, I snapped at her rump. At last she realised; with one last despairing, piping cry, she took off. Sick at heart, I retraced my steps to find the Platypus, who had not been able to keep up in the headlong chase.

'Thank you, Copper. You kept your word.' The voice, harsh and rasping, was one that I had not heard for a while.

I dipped my head. I could not bear to see the old hind's eyes.

96

'It wasn't much good.'

'You are wrong. You saved my daughter's life. She will have other babies. You could not have done more.' With that she turned, formidable in her dignity, graceful despite her age, and, with floating leaps, was gone.

But in spite of those forgiving words, I felt bad. Bad for the baby deer, helpless and outnumbered. Bad for his mother, robbed of her child, and bad for us dogs. The deer were protected by Royal decree, we all knew that. They weren't vermin, like squirrels or rabbits. The lurchers weren't even hungry; they did not need to kill to survive and they were not in any danger themselves. They were just gripped by bloodlust. I reckon to be as tough as the next dog, but I didn't like it. I had wanted to introduce the Platypus to the highways and byways of the park, but not like this. For a few days afterwards we were quite subdued and could not bring ourselves to go roaming.

But it is not in the nature of dogs to be sad for long, and before many days had passed the old wanderlust was coursing through my blood. Not only that, I was beginning to pick up, on the south wind, the tantalising scent of a bitch on heat. It was time to introduce the Platypus to the facts of life.

My nose told me to strike out across the park in the direction of Robin Hood Gate. Up Ham Gate Avenue, under the trees beside the road, and through Ham Gate. Into the park at Ham Cross, past Peg's Pond and Isabella Plantation, through Gibbet Wood and Prince Charles's Spinney, until we reached Robin Hood Gate. Just outside the gate was Stag Lodge Stables and there I had a collie girlfriend called Bella. I was pretty sure it was Bella's scent that I'd picked up on the wind, so we trotted in through the gates to see if we could find her. But the stables were quiet: hardly a horse or pony in sight and no Bella to be seen at all.

For a moment I was at a loss.

'What shall we do, Copper?' asked the Platypus, panting heavily.

'Wait for a new scent to come to us. Sniff the wind. See what you can pick up.'

Oh, how funny my dear Platypus looked with his tiny little legs and long body and his seal-shaped head lifted up to the wind. Needless to say, he picked up nothing. Nor, to be strictly truthful, did I to begin with but then suddenly came the unmistakable airborne message – sweet, pungent, intoxicating – from a bitch who was not only ready but impatient.

'I know,' I said, 'I bet it's old Ruby at Chessington. We'd better scamper on down there before she changes her mind.' This was, in fact, rather easier said than done. I had been to Chessington Zoo plenty of times with Mum and there had befriended Ruby, one of the keepers' dogs, but I had never tackled this extremely busy, dangerous stretch of road on my own before. As I looked up and down to see how we might manage it, I realised that on both sides of the highway there were good pavements with grass verges. It was a risk but I had to take it. The fever in my blood would not be denied.

'Come on, my boy,' I said, giving the Platypus a playful nudge. 'She's calling us. Time to get cracking.'

Crossing that road, with its dual carriageway and its roundabouts, took all my know-how and street cunning, I can tell you. I insisted that the Platypus stay as close to my side as if we were glued at the shoulder. Once over the road, heading south, I realised, with relief, that the pavement now stretched away in front of us and that nothing except a couple of miles of steady hound-jog stood between us and Ruby.

We had not gone very far when I became aware that one of the cars on the road kept slowing down to keep pace with us. The driver seemed to be looking out of the window at us. Now, when I had said to the Platypus that he mustn't make eye contact with strangers on our travels it was not just because it might land us in a fight or delay us along the way. It was also because I was afraid of being snatched. The canine world is full of kidnap stories: of dogs taken from cars, from outside shops and, above all, from the streets. I admit that the Platypus and I might not have been prime targets, owing to our mixed heritage, but lately there had been wild rumours of a thriving market in dog meat and I was always on my guard. You could not be too careful. The Platypus especially would probably have tasted pretty succulent if you liked that kind of thing.

To say that I didn't like the look of this car slowing down was an understatement. Frankly, I was poised for flight. The only trouble was this: if there was one thing the Platypus was not built for it was flight. He was already exhausted by trying to keep up with me on those preposterous little legs, and he also had a completely sweet and trusting nature. There is, as you know, a limit to what one wants to tell the young at any one time and I hadn't got around to the subject of dognapping or, even worse, dog meat. So when the car stopped and a woman got out, bent over the Platypus and said, in an admittedly sweet voice, 'Come, little chap. Are you lost?' he didn't hesitate. Utterly leg-weary and glad to be rescued, he allowed himself to be scooped up and put in the back of the car. What could I do? I could not let the Platypus go to an uncertain fate on his own. With great misgivings, I too jumped into the strange car – to find there not only the Platypus but also two golden retrievers.

'Hello,' said one of them. 'Coming to the shop with us?'

For a moment or two my imagination ran wild. A butcher's shop, specialising in dog meat? A fur shop, selling coats made out of dog skin? A pet shop, where the Platypus would be put in a cage and sold to the highest bidder?

'You all right?' said the other retriever. 'Not carsick, are you?'

'No I am not,' I said indignantly, forgetting my fears for a second. 'Never been carsick in my life.'

'Good, can't stand dogs who puke.' With that we lapsed into silence. We all knew that human beings don't like dog noise in cars and there seemed nothing much to say. Either we were in safe hands or we weren't. We would soon know.

After some time – I really don't know how long – we pulled up. I knew that we had left London a while ago and now the first thing I heard as our driver opened her door was the crying of gulls, wheeling in great squadrons overhead.

I whispered to the Platypus, 'As soon as she opens the door, follow me.'

'What do you mean to do?' asked the poor little fellow, clearly longing to stay put and go on resting his tired legs.

'Get away from here. Find our way back to Mum somehow.' As I spoke, the boot door opened and I pushed the Platypus out, half jumping on top of him as I launched myself out as well. But it was no good. The Platypus – even if he had not been tired – was not the dog for speedy getaways and our kindly persecutor had grabbed him before he could even get to his feet. Once again I was trapped.

At least the shop into which we were taken did not seem to sell meat, fur or pets. Instead it was stuffed with furniture and ornaments. A bit like Ormeley but more higgledy-piggledy, with things stacked on top of each other.

'Antiques. Very valuable. We guard them for her, you know,' said one of the retrievers.

'It's all right, Copper, isn't it?' said the Platypus anxiously. 'We can stay for a bit? I'm awfully tired.'

'Yes,' I said reluctantly. 'It doesn't seem too bad. We'll rest for a while. But then we must get on the road home. I can't break my promise to Mum about getting back before dark.'

I was frankly still worried about the intentions of our dog-napper. I might have been off the mark about meat and fur and suchlike but, as a gentleman of the road, I knew all about do-gooders with romantic ideas of taking in rescue dogs. Before long my worst fears had been realised. Putting down a dish of food, which we were too hungry to resist, the woman proceeded to take our collars off. I might have guessed! Without them we were nameless, homeless strays. She was going to destroy our identities.

'Quick, Platypus. Eat up. We *must* go.'

And now he too was ready. Without a backward glance, nose glued to my tail, he followed me as I raced for the door. We were free! Oh what a relief it was to sniff the good fresh air and inhale the salty smell of the sea. Mum had by now taken me often enough to the seaside for me to know that this town was right on the coast. Following my nose, we wound our way through the streets until, sure enough, we found ourselves on the seafront. Intoxicated by the air, heady with the knowledge that we were our own masters again, I scampered down to the shore.

'Copper,' called the Platypus. 'Copper, steady. I can't keep up.'

But I was selfish. I could smell adventures, I could hear the noise of fairground music, see the bright, coloured lights of a merry-go-round. Now that we were here, I could not resist having a little fun. What happened next was entirely my fault.

'Let's go to the fair,' I called carelessly over my shoulder as I ran on to the pier, smelling that heavenly mixture of hot dogs and chips, candyfloss, ice cream, popcorn and old cooking fat. Oh the brightness, the exhilarating swirl of the music! I loved it.

By the time I looked around for the Platypus, it was too late. He was nowhere to be seen. Even then I didn't turn back. I could smell a bitch somewhere near by. It was too much to resist. She was ready, I was willing. I cannot tell you much about her. Whatever memories there might have been were blotted out by what came next.

Trotting back the way I came, looking everywhere for the Platypus, I was halfway up the beach when the most dreadful sight met my eyes. Some boys were holding something between them attached to two long pieces of string. The game, being applauded by a couple of onlookers, was a kind of tug of war. The object being pulled apart by the strings tied to his front and back legs was the Platypus.

'Let's see if he can fly,' shouted one of his persecutors.

'Those legs are no good, that's for sure,' said another, beginning to whirl the Platypus round and round.

With more speed and strength than I ever knew I had and a silent prayer to the fighting spirit of my ancestors, I launched myself through the air at the boy nearest me. If I had got him, I would have killed him. Luckily I did not. From behind me came a roar.

'Stand still!' It was a parade-ground bark such as I had only ever heard on television before, and it stopped every one of us in our tracks. The boys dropped the string, then took to their heels, the Platypus flopped on to the beach and I came to rest beside him.

'What's all this? Bloody boys!'

A burly old man stood there with a stick. He was dressed in a blazer with burnished buttons and his shoes had toecaps so shiny you could see your face in them. He stooped down to stroke the Platypus, murmuring gruffly, 'Poor little chap, poor little chap.'

I probably should not have done it, but I growled. I'm sorry about it now. He had come to our rescue, but I wasn't taking any chances.

'All right, old boy. All right. I won't hurt you.'

I growled again, even more fiercely, and this time he got the message. With a regretful last look at us both he turned to walk away, straight-backed and dignified, like the fine soldier he had obviously once been.

The Platypus was still lying unmoving on the shingle. Wearily, wretchedly, I began to lick his face, hoping he was alive but knowing in my heart that he was not.

But my dear, dear son, the Platypus, was made of sterner stuff than I had supposed. With a sudden sneeze as I licked his nose, he opened his eyes.

'Oh, Copper,' he gasped, 'that wasn't a very nice game. Can we go home now?'

'Yes, we certainly can,' I said. 'The sooner the better.'

It was easier said than done, though. The Platypus not only had his legs tied up with string, he was also completely exhausted.

'Right,' I said, 'you start chewing at the stuff on your front legs and I'll do the back.' It was a long and tedious job. The light was fading from the sky and a chilly wind had sprung up, whipping the grey water into little waves and making the cables on the funfair machinery flap and bang about. There was hardly anyone around now, only the odd homeless drunk and a couple of teenage boys idly kicking an empty tin can. No one paid any attention to us as we huddled together, wondering how on earth we would ever get home.

We were beginning to give up hope, when, in the distance, faint but unmistakable, we heard a cry, 'Copper, Platypus! Copper, Copper!'

Mum? No, not Mum but the antique-selling dog-napper, walking along the beach and holding out our collars, telling us that Mum was anxiously waiting for us at home. I had got the wrong end of the stick. She had only wanted our collars for the telephone number and the names engraved on them. I can honestly say that I have never been gladder to see anyone in my life.

Mum said she couldn't believe we had made it all the way to Brighton, but looking back it is clear to me that our trip was the beginning of the end of my adventures with the Platypus. I did go on plenty more excursions but he could never keep up and gradually I learned to leave him at about midday on friendly doorsteps, hoping that the house owner would ring Mum and that she would fetch him. One day Jessie said 'Look Copper, I don't know if you realise what's going on but Mum's found the Platypus a new home. In the country.'

Part of me was sadder than I can possibly tell you. Part of me was relieved. In the end, love him as I did, his safety was more to me than anything. When we said goodbye for the last time, we knew that we would never forget each other. We were father and son and no distance on earth could change that.

8

THE TRIAL

There are some who would say that up until now I had led a charmed life. Jessie would have put it another way and said I was heading for a fall. Not that she would have known much about that. She always fell on her feet. But the truth is that in this life of ours no one gets away completely scot free. Not even Jessie. And now bleak times were ahead for Ormeley.

The first bad thing was that Mum's eldest pup, Rupert, disappeared and was never seen again. I wished with all my heart that I had been able to speak human language during this time. Mum's way of coping was not to talk about it: to shut down all her feelings and carry on with whatever she had to do. But you cannot hide things from a dog. I daresay you can't hide things from cats either, in fact, I know to my cost that you cannot. It's just that they've mastered the trick of not seeming to care so much about their human owners.

But I did care. I hated Mum being unhappy, yet there was no way that I could tell her the most important thing of all: you will get used to it. You won't get over it but you will get used to it. We dogs know that better than anyone. I got used to losing my mother, I got used to being parted from the Platypus: I got used to these sad things because I had to.

I can't pretend, however, that I made it my life's mission to comfort Mum night and day. I was a dog in the prime of my life and at the height of my strength. The truth was that I was arrogant – probably a bit more arrogant than our mother intended when she advised us to carry ourselves with pride. I had become something of a law unto myself. I had complete freedom and yet I also had complete security. I am afraid it is a mixture that would go to any dog's head. Although it grieves me to admit it, it went to mine. I had made many friends but I had also made some enemies, the most deadly of which was the keeper's dog, who lived at the lodge. We hated each other with a total passion and would have fought to the death if our owners had let us. If you ask me why we hated each other so much, I would have to reply that I'm not sure. It was just a personality clash but a clash of such ferocity that one or the other of us would not have come out of any serious fight alive.

There were also other forces at work after Rupert's

disappearance. For one thing, there was the mighty hurricane which uprooted some of the most ancient trees in the park. Roofs came off sheds, garden fences blew down, and all the villains in the area – canine, feline and human – were free to roam as they pleased all night long. It was a time of wildness and chaos and it set fire to my blood. I still kept my promise not to leave Ormeley at night, but sometimes the call was too strong and I would join a family of foxes that regularly played on the lawn in the early hours of the morning, before daybreak.

At first Ormeley itself seemed to have escaped the worst of the hurricane but, unknown to any of us, the foundations of the great wall which separated our garden from the golf course had become weakened by the storm, and a second storm, a little later, brought it crashing down. Now there was nothing to hold me and I made the most of it. But the reverse was also true: there was nothing to stop enemy dogs or people invading Ormeley.

At the same time something extraordinary happened in the sky, which affected all the magnetic paths by which we animals travel. The moon quite literally stood still. I first noticed it one summer night when patrolling the garden. While the wall was down I had taken to playing night watchman and now I saw that the full moon seemed to be hanging just above the treetops. I had never seen it so low. Night after clear night, as it waned, I marvelled at how close it seemed – just as if I could jump up and take a bite out of it. I asked the collies what was going on.

'I think – though I'm not quite sure, mind you –' said

Flora, 'that this is what the old shepherds at the farm sometimes talked about. I seem to remember our mother mentioning it.'

'You could be right,' said Tessa thoughtfully, 'They used to say that when the moon stood still like this, then the earth's magnetic paths would join up.'

'Really?' I felt a prickle of anticipation run all the way along my spine from neck to tail.

'But you must be careful, Copper. Too much power under your feet can truly lead you astray. Please, please be careful.'

'Yes, yes, I promise,' I lied, desperate to get out and see what adventures would happen to me.

Now, I do not know if it was the moon, the stars or just plain coincidence, but I can tell you that this time was one of quite extraordinary excitement for me: there was hardly a suburb within reach that I didn't investigate. Mum had of course wisely given me complete freedom, but even so I could tell that she sometimes worried when friend after friend telephoned to say that I had been seen in Kingston, Surbiton, East Molesey and innumerable other places.

She would have worried even more if she had known that my secret vice – biting joggers and sometimes cyclists – was also getting well and truly out of control. I know I haven't said much about this before – I suppose you will say that, like all addicts, human or canine, I was in denial and you would of course be right. But it is also true to say that up until now I had got away with it and mostly it did not reach

Mum's ears. However, all that was about to change and with it my entire existence.

Only I know the whole truth and nothing but the truth, so I might as well tell you everything just as it happened. I am happy to throw my paws in the air and confess that I bit many people but the offence for which I almost lost my life was not entirely my fault.

Occasionally, when I was on the right side of the big wrought-iron front gates, watching the world go by, two nasty boys with an even nastier father would taunt me through the bars, poking sticks at me and driving me into a frenzy of rage. I admit that I snarled and snapped but, after all, I was there to guard my home and family. Not only that, those boys reminded me of that terrible day in Brighton with the Platypus. These incidents occurred on a regular basis and you should have heard the language that accompanied them. It is quite unrepeatable here, but suffice it to say that 'filthy mutt' and 'dirty mongrel' were the mildest of the insults. The cowards knew they were safe as long as those iron bars were between us.

Then one day I had had enough. The tauntings generally took place around teatime, I imagine because the father collected his sons from school first, then walked past our gate. I decided that I would keep them under observation from the nearby woods and thus be one jump ahead of them.

After about a week of this, my patience was rewarded. I saw the three of them armed with sticks, waiting for me at the gate. I leapt out from the bushes, with my lips drawn back in the most ferocious snarl I could manage. Teeth bared, I tore the stick from one of the boys' hands. They all turned to run away in terror, so I grabbed my chief tormentor's trousers. Fortunately for me they were very thick and, although I bit him as hard as I could, my teeth barely touched the skin of his fat leg. As I prepared to give chase, I heard Jessie's voice from the wall, 'Stop, Copper! Don't do that! They're not worth it. They usually throw sticks and stones at me too but I just duck. Please come away.'

Reluctantly I stopped in my tracks. Although I hate to admit it, Jessie is often wiser than I am.

Time passed and I had almost forgotten about this episode until, one morning at breakfast, Mum was opening her mail. Among the envelopes was a long brown one. Whatever was inside it caused her to cry out in dismay. 'Oh God!' she said, 'It's a summons. Copper's bitten someone and I'm being prosecuted for owning a dangerous dog. They've reported it to the police.'

At first I was truculent. The cheek of it! But then it began to dawn on me that this was serious. Perhaps the most serious trouble I had ever been in. Mum talked endlessly on the telephone to her brother Alastair at his home in Dorset. It seemed that the crime carried with it the death penalty. At first I thought it was one of Mum's little jokes but then I saw a tear roll down her cheek. I slunk out of the room, my tail between my legs. I went to find the collies.

'I've bitten someone in the driveway,' I said plaintively. 'But that man and those two boys were teasing me with sticks. Anyway, I didn't bite the boy. His trousers were too thick and Jessie stopped me going after him.'

'Copper!' said Tessa. 'You've made the biggest mistake of your life. Dogs are not allowed to bite humans, the law says so. They can do anything they like to you, but if you retaliate you get punished.'

'The worst part is that you could be taken away from Mum,' said Flora. 'She loves you, which means she will be punished too.'

I went back to the house feeling very depressed. What Flora and Tessa had told me really worried me and I had no desire to go out that day or in the days that followed. I felt really nervous and because I didn't properly understand the words I overheard – words like 'law', 'magistrates', 'court' and 'prosecution' – I made up my mind to stick as close to Mum as I could and keep my ears open.

As the days passed I learned that Mum had acquired the services of a barrister, whose job it would be to defend me in court when the case came up. She was also busy collecting witnesses to testify to my good nature. She was going to call Lorna, the lovely lady who looked after us all when Mum was away, also a man called Doug Hill, father of Jemima's best friend Becky, who was a great dog lover and a great pal of mine. Mum was also collecting letters from admirers like Jilly Cooper, who had promised to testify on my behalf. I just hoped that Barbara Woodhouse did not get wind of the trial.

Once or twice I made a half-hearted attempt to go wandering in Richmond Park, but I took no pleasure in it. Instead I found myself following Mum around the house and I had an absurd urge to curl up on her lap like Jessie did. My uneasiness seemed to be infectious: Tessa and Flora were on edge, constantly fighting with each other over trivial matters and Jessie had stopped biting my head off. Instead, I would catch her watching me rather anxiously. When I wasn't following Mum around the house, I would play ball with the children in the garden and sometimes, because it was summer, we would all have a swim in the pool.

One day, as the whole household was waiting tensely for my fate to be decided, a surprise visitor arrived at Ormeley. Like Tessa and Flora, he arrived in a big cardboard box and was a present from Mum's first mate, Mark. His name was Jasper and he was utterly adorable, a spaniel-labrador cross, fat and roly poly, with long soft ears and the most helpless, appealing expression in his large eyes.

If anything could have cheered me up, consoled me for the loss of the Platypus and made me forget the impending court case, it was Jasper. All my paternal feelings were aroused once more and I immediately wanted to show him the ropes and teach him how to go roving with me.

But Mum, already very worried about me, was wiser than I was on this occasion. She absolutely forbade anyone to let Jasper follow me out of the gardens at Ormeley. He was too young, she said, and not streetwise like me.

Jessie said 'Of course Mum won't risk him. You know why he's come, don't you?'

'Well, yes. To be a friend for me.'

'Sometimes you can be very dense, Copper,' she said impatiently. 'He's here in case you aren't, once the court case is over.'

'Do you truly think it will come to that, Jessie?'

'Yes, I do. You've been a complete fool, Copper. Better prepare yourself for the worst.'

Now, I don't hold with friends being two-faced and I would much rather have something nasty said to my face than behind my back. But there are limits and so I told Jessie to shut up in no uncertain terms. It was my life on the line, not hers, and she had no business to talk to me as though she had never done anything wrong in her life. I decided not to talk to her any more.

Instead I devoted myself to Jasper, willing the days to pass so that he could be strong enough to travel with me. I knew that when he was fully grown he would be bigger than me, being half labrador, and that he would be quite able to look after himself in a way that the Platypus had not been. But the bad luck which seemed to haunt Ormeley these days was about to envelop Jasper too.

Mum had gone to a horse show with Jemima, leaving me in charge of Jasper. Secretly I planned to nip out for a couple of hours to teach him some road sense, but Mimi had been given strict instructions to watch me. 'Whatever you do, Mimi, I beg you not to let Jasper anywhere near the gates,' said Mum before she left for the day. 'They could open at any time and it would be instant death if he got out on to the road. Let him play in the garden but, please, please, Mimi, keep an eye on him.'

But Mimi could not keep an eye on us every second of the day, as I knew full well, and it was the work of a moment once her attention was diverted to slip through the gates, with Jasper at my heels.

Once on Ham Gate Avenue, I repeated the lesson that I had taught the Platypus. Roads are for cars, lorries and bikes, not for dogs. Stick to the pavement or grass verge, whatever you do. Watch how I cross the road at the lights. Wait for the traffic to stop. If in doubt, copy other dogs and their owners.

But whereas the Platypus had been very biddable and pretty quick on the uptake, Jasper was not. He was over-excitable and independent-minded. Time after time, as we trotted down Ham Gate Avenue, I had to tell him to stick with me. As luck would have it, there was no traffic for the first few hundred yards. But then our luck ran out. Jasper, with a naughty look at me over his shoulder, bounded into the middle of the road and into the path of an oncoming car. He didn't stand a chance.

I don't know how long I stood there, licking his face, hoping against hope that he would open his eyes just as the Platypus had done on the beach at Brighton. All I do know is that at first I would not let anyone near his body: not the driver who had killed him; not the vet who happened to be in the car behind; not even Zac, who had come running out of Ormeley to see what had happened. But at last I knew that it was no good. Jasper had gone. Tears were running down Zac's face as he bent over him.

'Come away, Copper,' he said, 'there's nothing you can do. I'm afraid he's dead.'

I allowed him to gather Jasper up and together we walked back to the house. I had my head down and my tail between my legs. I could not bear to look at Jasper's puppy face, with

118

its long ears dangling over Zac's arm. I knew it was I, not the driver of the car, who had killed him.

And now the day that I had been dreading had arrived. Mum was taking no chances. I heard her talking to Alastair. 'Keep him in the back of your car, Al,' she said, 'and I will ring you from the court and let you know the verdict. If it goes against us, drive like hell back to Dorset.'

I had never seen her face so grim.

'Good luck, Professor,' said Alastair, as he put me in his car. He always called me that because he said my beard gave me a scholarly look. I sat on the back seat of Alastair's car while he flung suitcases into the boot. He had the use of a flat over the garages and occasionally I was invited in for a biscuit. He had a wire-haired fox-terrier bitch called Dixie. Although I never fancied her, she was a good mate. However, much as I liked them both, I did not really care for the idea of making a new life in Dorset. I mean, the country is all right for a quick visit – a weekend, maybe – but I knew that I would miss street life. Ormeley and Richmond Park were quite rural enough for me. I agreed with Jimmy, who once said to Mum, 'Darling, can't you understand? After a few hours in the country, every blade of grass becomes a personal enemy.'

I must have fallen asleep for a while because, when I woke up, the big white gates of Ormeley were opening and Mum's car was coming in. As I peered out anxiously, I saw Mum, Lorna and Alastair standing in the yard, laughing and looking happy. Mum let me out of the car and hugged me. 'Oh Copper, you bad, bad fellow,' she said, half-laughing, half-crying. 'You don't know what you've put us through. Everything's got to change now. No more roaming. From now on it's home sweet home for you.'

I must say I didn't quite like the sound of the last bit, but I was so happy to see her happy that I leapt about, jumping up at everyone and trying to lick their faces. Later, while everyone was having tea, I sat by the table and heard what had taken place that day. Mum said to Alastair, 'You can't imagine how funny it was when the magistrates looked at the photographs.'

'What photographs?'

'Oh, the ones my lawyer told me to take of the place where the offence happened. I couldn't resist slipping one in of Copper dressed in his Mafia outfit and that sweet one of him with Jessie. I thought they would show him as a real family pet.'

She showed the photos to Alastair, who thought they were extremely funny.

'But it wasn't all funny,' she went on. 'I was so worried at the time because you never know how these cases will turn out. Although Lorna and Doug were brilliant witnesses and both stressed how good-natured Cooper was, I was terrified the other side would produce some stranger who would say he'd been bitten by Copper in the park. That horrible man and one of his sons sat on the other side of the court and glared at me. I'm sure they were disappointed with the verdict. I think they really wanted Copper put down.'

'So what *was* the verdict?' asked Alastair.

'Copper is not to be allowed off the premises unless he is

on the lead, accompanied by one of us. We've got to pay quite a heavy fine and he has to have a little operation to stop him hankering after the bitches.'

All this sounded dismal to me. Was I really condemned to spending all my days at home, playing in the garden? What about my girlfriends? Was I never to have a romp with them again? More to the point, what about this little operation? I was not sure I liked the sound of that at all. I wandered out into the garden and found Jessie sunning herself on the terrace. I described the day's events to her and mentioned as casually as I could that there was talk of a little operation.

'Oh,' she said, wide awake now. 'Did they say what kind of operation?'

'Not exactly. Just that it would help me stay at home.'

'Ah. That sort of operation.'

'Come on, Jessie, don't tease.'

'I think,' she said, cleaning her paws and rolling on to her back, 'I think it's probably the same as what they do to male cats. It's called neutering.' She gave me a sly look out of her slanting green eyes. I had a nasty feeling she was secretly laughing.

'What's that?' I said.

'Well now,' said Jessie annoyingly, pretending to pounce on an imaginary mouse, 'that's for me to know and you to find out.'

9

A NEW LIFE

I intend to draw a polite veil over the days immediately following the trial. Let's just say that I was never again the dog I had once been and leave it at that.

It was probably a good thing that the fierce longing to stray which had driven me all my life now began to ebb away. It would be untrue to say that I didn't miss my freedom. I missed it very much. Or perhaps I missed the status it gave me. To know that I could go wherever I wanted, whenever I wanted, was the most precious feeling in the world.

In the canine world there are domestic dogs and there are feral dogs. Each has things the other cannot have. Domestic dogs have regular food, warmth and safety but are entirely

125

reliant on their owners for exercise and liberty. Feral dogs have all the exercise and freedom anyone could want but they live on the edge, almost always hungry, often cold and wet, seldom loved.

I, on the other hand, had the best of both those worlds. I had food, warmth, safety and love. But I also had a territory that ranged the length and breadth of south London. Part rural, part urban, full of beautiful bitches of all shapes and sizes, my territory was scattered with good friends, human and canine, from every walk of life. In these recollections I have only been able to give you the merest taste of what it was like. I was a lucky dog, make no mistake about it.

So, if you ask me what I disliked most about the sentence that had been imposed on me, I would have to say it was the embarrassment. Sometimes, in the pubs I went to, I would hear men talking about losing their jobs. It was not the loss of money which they minded, so much as the loss of self-respect. They had lost the idea of who they were and what they were for. It was a bit the same with me. Copper the rover, the stud dog, the canny traveller – that Copper had gone. I was still me, but a different me.

Now I could only walk up Ham Gate Avenue on a lead with Mum. She did let me off when we reached the woods in Richmond Park, and there I was allowed to chase squirrels to my heart's content. Nevertheless, after half an hour or so, I could be sure of hearing her calling me, her voice getting shriller, with that note of annoyance creeping in which I knew so well. You'd have thought that she would have been able to hear me dashing from tree to tree, barking at the squirrels that kept frustratingly out of my reach. But apparently not.

Inevitably I lost touch with some friends, like Toby for instance, but I did get quite a few visitors at Ormeley, so my social life was not at a complete standstill. Bungle was a regular.

'No one could tell there's anything different about you,' he said loyally one afternoon. He really was a good chap and although it was only natural that he should be secretly pleased to see my wanderings restricted, he was much too nice to say so. And, of course, this kind of life was the only one he had ever known so it was no big deal for him.

But the biggest shock for me was that, unexpectedly, Tessa and Flora had got old, and, with this sudden ageing, their characters changed. Instead of the faithful mentors who always had a wise opinion on everything, they became sad and crotchety. I am ashamed to tell you that I began to avoid their company. I had two new friends who were much more fun: sleek grey whippets called Chester and Arnie, a father and son.

They belonged to Robin, the second of Mum's litter. They would arrive every weekend, barely greeting me before tearing round and round the garden at a speed you cannot imagine. I would attempt to join in but they were much faster than me and, of course, although I hate to admit it, much younger and fitter. Finally exhausted, they would collapse on to the lawn and we would have a chat. I felt envious of the life they described because, although they lived in London, they told me they were allowed as much freedom as they wanted when out on their walks.

'I've been in trouble with the police, you know,' Chester said proudly. 'Pack of lies, of course. A policewoman said I'd frightened her horse and bitten it on the nose. I mean, really, as if I would!'

I was agog. 'What happened then?'

'Oh, it went to court, of course,' he said airily. 'But they didn't stand a chance. I had dozens of witnesses on my side. The main one was that famous dog psychologist chap, Roger Mugford.'

I had never heard of the fellow, but didn't want to say so. Chester really was the most conceited chap and a terrible boaster. You could say that it takes one to know one, but really the stories he told were outrageous. Apparently he had fathered hundreds of whippet puppies already, had chased deer in the park with Arnie, without getting caught, and never had to be on a lead.

'You could be shot, you know, Chester. It's against the law to chase deer. Does Robin know about this?'

'I expect so,' said Chester, stretching himself out on the lawn. 'You may be right, Copper old boy, but I don't really give a toss.'

This did not sound right to me and I privately wondered if Chester was making the whole thing up. But there was no stopping him.

'Robin doesn't often walk with us because he's too busy but, even if he did, he'd never stop us doing something we wanted to do, nor would Samantha our dog walker.'

'Hmm,' I said. If it was true, then it was very unfair.

One week later I learned the truth. In the morning I was

showing off my diving skills in the swimming pool with the children and noticed out of the corner of my eye that neither of the whippets seemed keen to join in, in spite of my encouragement. 'We can't be bothered,' they said, speaking with one voice as they often did. They sat watching me from under the shady tree by the pool and I noticed that, whatever position they sat or lay in, they looked as graceful as statues. Posing, I called it, and if you wanted to be mean you could have thought they looked rather like overgrown grey mice.

That afternoon, Mum and her friend Jean Gardiner took the whippets and me for a walk, along with Jean's two spaniels Ben and Sam. We walked down to Pen Ponds, where the spaniels and I dashed into the water and chased after the ducks. Mum had let me off the lead and after our swim I ran into the bracken with Ben and Sam. I turned round to see if Chester and Arnie were following us and saw that they were still on long stretch leads.

How come? I wondered and then I heard Mum say to Jean, 'Robin has told me never to let the whippets off the lead in Richmond Park. It's too dangerous with all the deer around. Samantha is only allowed to let them off one at a time in Kensington Gardens.'

As they both strained and pulled on their leads, I could not help whispering to Arnie, 'Going to catch any deer today?' before tearing off to catch up with the spaniels and find a squirrel or two. For once Chester, proud as he was, looked so embarrassed that I felt sorry for him. I brought Arnie a dead squirrel to make up for it, pretending that I had just caught it, but judging by the smell it must have been dead for weeks, though I don't think he was any the wiser.

Sometime after this there came the third change in my life. The first was my rescue, the second the curtailment of my freedom and this was the third.

Tessa and Flora were undoubtedly going steadily down-hill; they were now very old and spent lots of time at the vet, for which I pitied them as I hated going. At home they lay around, listless, barely bothering to eat their dinner. I worried about them but I did not really understand how ill they were. One morning I awoke to the sound of Flora howling: a sound so alien and strange that I rushed into the laundry room. There, lying in her basket, was Tessa; she looked very peaceful, as if she was sleeping. I sniffed her.

'Copper,' wept Flora, 'Tessa has gone.'

'Gone where?' I said, bewildered.

'She's dead,' said Flora.

It was my first experience of an adult dog death and it upset me a lot. I watched Mum and Lorna show Tessa's body to the vet and saw him shake his head. 'Poor old girl,' he said. 'But what a wonderful age she reached and what a peaceful way to go.'

Mum held a funeral service for her in a corner of the garden where the snowdrops grow in winter. A little stone was placed there marking her grave and showing her name and birth date. I used to visit it, wondering where she had really gone, unable to believe that I would never see her again.

Shortly after this, Flora pined away and died too. In spite

of their constant bickering, she could not live without her sister and joined Tessa among the snowdrops and the camellia bushes.

I felt curiously bereft without Tessa and Flora. I was never quite as close to them as I had been to the Platypus or to Bungle, but they had been a constant part of my life since I had arrived at Ormeley and things seemed slightly unreal without them. I expect I was suffering from only-dog syndrome. Maybe I looked more disconsolate than I really felt, because everyone kept making a fuss of me. I constantly heard people saying how lonely I looked and how Mum ought to get another dog to keep me company.

I am not sure whether I agreed with that but, at any rate, one day Mum went missing for hours and when she returned she was holding something in her hands which looked rather like a small teddy bear. She placed it on the lawn where, exactly as I had done to much applause as a puppy, it squatted down and had a pee. Having done so, it ran round and round in excited circles without showing the slightest sign of nerves. I had never seen anything quite so cocky and when I sniffed him by way of an introduction, he gave a playful little growl.

His name was Barney and he was a Norfolk terrier. He was so small that I felt protective of him, though why I cannot think as anything less in need of protection I cannot imagine. Jessie, after several wrestling attempts that knocked her clean off her feet, smacked him as hard as she could to put him in his place. It was no good; he continued to advance, growling playfully, and trying to encircle her neck with his mouth. That first slap had been with claws sheathed but then she lashed out at him with her claws fully extended. He ran away howling, but we knew he would be back for more.

'Oh bother,' Jessie said to me. 'That one's never going to learn. Give him an inch and he'll take a yard. Mark my words, he means to be master.'

'What d'you mean?' I said. 'He's only tiny.'

She sniffed. 'Just you wait and see. Tiny or not, he will end up top dog.'

In fact, for the first year of his life, Barney and I rubbed along quite happily, particularly on our walks. We both chased squirrels and rabbits and, although I was definitely not as quick as I had been in my youth, he seemed indefatigable just as I had been at his age.

'He's only a puppy,' Mum would say soothingly to me, stroking my head. 'You'll see, he'll soon settle down.' He didn't. In every way he could, he tried to dominate me and it took endless patience on my part to ignore him.

One year later Mum bought him a mate, another Norfolk terrier called Bee. She was a completely different character from Barney: sweet and gentle but, at the same time, sporting. I loved her and, when Barney was out of sight, we would sneak off together for a chat. She flirted with me outrageously, much to Barney's fury, as she constantly licked me and rolled on her back in front of me.

'Bee,' I would tell her, 'I really like you, but you don't belong to me; you are Barney's mate, or at least you're supposed to be.'

Of course I had rather lost my enthusiasm for the kind of loving that Barney and Bee were supposed to be indulging in, but Bee never did seem to get the message. Barney, on the other hand, found her very attractive and was extremely jealous of me. I wanted to tell him to whip her off somewhere quiet and give her a right good seeing-to and I guess that is exactly what he must have done because, the following year, Bee produced four puppies. I was really proud of her, and watching her as she nursed her young gave me nostalgic memories of lying sheltered by my mother's side. Barney didn't seem particularly interested in his puppies, so I was able to keep a watchful eye on them without incurring his jealousy.

The warm weather meant that they spent the days outside in a run in the garden but I didn't like the way the crows used to land on the lawn and look at them as though they were juicy titbits. Bee and I talked quite a bit that summer about their future. 'I am only allowed to keep one,' she said matter-of-factly. 'Mum has found good homes for the other three.'

But it did not work out that way. Mum decided to keep two of the puppies after all: Boris, the only male, and a funny little black-and-tan bitch, who had not got on well in the new home she went to.

'That little black one is the pick of the bunch,' I told Bee. 'She has more guts than all the others put together.'

I was right. She grew up to be a sporting little thing and Mum named her Bindy. And so life went on and, although my bones were beginning to creak a bit and I was stiffer in my movements, I did have fun with the little Norfolks. Naturally I could not discuss any of my weaknesses with Barney, because he would have taken advantage. As it was, he had taken to nipping my legs when we were running across the garden. I didn't want him to guess that I was finding it harder and harder to hear Mum calling me. In my heart of hearts I knew I was losing my hearing.

Once or twice I did lose my temper with Barney. On one occasion Mum was throwing clumps of seaweed for me on the beach in Cornwall, where she took us on holiday. Loving the sea as I did, I would tear into the waves to retrieve it, shaking the seaweed like a rat. Barney, little show-off that he was, decided to join in. Tugging it between us, at first playfully and then more seriously, we got into a fight. Although older, I was bigger and stronger and could have killed him, but he just would not give up. Mum picked me up by the scruff of the neck, with Barney hanging from my jaws, and I was forced to drop him. Incandescent with rage, he danced round in a fury, and I told him to get lost. Within minutes it was all forgotten but it was important. A line had been crossed. Barney now saw himself as top dog.

Nevertheless, we were still allies on our walks and there was one never-to-be-forgotten day when I had cause to be deeply grateful for the guts and tenacity of the Norfolks.

I had grown up with the deer in the park; I had made my peace with them and I always treated them with respect, especially the red deer. The hinds were particularly dangerous when they had young at foot, but the Norfolks were not as careful as I was. Perhaps they needed to be taught a lesson, just as I had been on my very first excursion into deer territory. At any rate, they would quite often chase the deer, and one day, as we were wandering through the woods, I must have got between a hind and her young by mistake. Normally I would have picked up the lightest rustle in the leaves, but my hearing was now so poor that I heard nothing.

A savage blow to my spine was the first I knew of the mortal danger I was in. I turned my head and saw the most terrifying sight: the hind with her front legs poised for the final killing strike. Nothing could save me, I knew that. I could not count the dogs who had been killed over the years in this way.

But I had reckoned without the Norfolks. Racing towards me in a pack, they flew as one at the hind and unbalanced her until, unnerved, she turned and ran, with her baby behind her. When Mum arrived on the scene she found me still on the ground, surrounded by the faithful terriers. Luckily I was only bruised and a few days rest soon saw me on my feet again. But it taught me an important lesson, one which, as a born loner, I had never had to learn before. We may have been different from one another – and had our differences – but in the end the Ormeley dogs were a pack and would defend each other to the death.

10

THE END

It is the strangest feeling being able to see one's own body lying in the gutter, silent, still and covered in blood. I barely saw and certainly did not hear the car which came out of the misty darkness and ended my life. I can remember seeing lights but hearing nothing, feeling a violent blow, a momentary savage pain and then only blackness. Yet, coming out of this oblivion, here I was, looking at myself lying shrunken and crumpled like one of those crushed foxes I had so often seen lying by the side of the road in the past.

How odd that it should have ended just as Jessie foretold. At the last, without my hearing, all my hard-won road sense, my enormous experience as a traveller, were no good to me at all. I saw the car driver looking at me, nudging my body with his foot and then getting back into his car and waiting. He could not see me standing in front of him and I could not understand why. Then at last I saw a familiar car driving up the avenue and now I could actually hear, for the first time in years, a beloved voice calling me, 'Copper! Copper!'

The car drove away, turned and came back. Mum and Isabel jumped out. I wagged my tail and tried to jump up at Mum, but she did not seem to register. Instead she bent over the dead animal lying by the side of the road and cried and cried. Isabel was crying too, but Mum was inconsolable. I tried to comfort her. I said, 'It's all right, Mum. I'm here. That's not me lying there, it's some other dog.' But she could not hear me.

Mum and Isabel tenderly gathered up the wretched carcass that they seemed to think was me and wrapped it in the car rug to take to Ormeley. I trotted along behind the car. When they arrive home, I thought to myself, surely the Norfolks will see me, but they didn't. They gathered round the corpse and Bee howled.

'Pull yourself together, Bee,' I said, quite sharply, annoyed that I seemed to be invisible, but she didn't seem to understand. Even she could not see or hear me. Mum stood in the hall and later a policeman came. I sat wagging my tail and generally trying to be ingratiating. I have always found it useful to keep in with the police. But there was no response from him, either.

'I am very sorry, madam,' he said, 'but the driver needs your insurance details.'

'What insurance details?' asked Mum, looking tear-stained and startled.

'Well, madam, when your dog was hit, I am afraid he did some damage to the car.' His voice sounded apologetic, rather than accusatory.

'Damage?' said Mum. 'How could a little dog like Copper damage a big car?' She saw by the policeman's face that he was sympathetic, but that he had to do his duty.

'Very well,' she said and went up the stairs to get the relevant documents. I could tell by the set of her back that she was outraged.

You bastard, I thought to myself, meaning the driver. All right, it was my fault for being in the road, but how many times have I seen a car driving up Ham Gate Avenue going like a bat out of hell? How many foxes and squirrels have I seen flattened and now look what's happened?

After the policeman had left, expressing his condolences as he went, Mum went off to ring Alastair, her closest confidant. I was sitting by her side. My head was on her knee but she did not feel it and finally I began to understand. I was here only in spirit, while my body lay outside. I could feel now that I was being pulled away by something that I didn't quite understand, but I needed to listen and hear what happened to me before I left Ormeley for ever.

I was fifteen, one hundred and five in dog years and a great age. Deaf as a post, admittedly, but still young at heart. Many friends had gone before me: Flora and Tessa, of course; Jessie who died in her sleep one sunny afternoon, too old and tired to scold any more, and Jimmy, to whom I became very close in the end. Apart from my daily walks, which I had still enjoyed, my life had centred around Mum's bedroom. Every night, and occasionally in the daytime, I would lie on her big sofa, wrapped up in my new duvet. I used to have an old one, belonging to Ben, with trains on it – something to do with Thomas the Tank Engine, I think. But I had had a new one, made by Colefax and Fowler, to match Mum's room.

Every night Mum had wrapped me up like a pancake and given me a kiss on the nose. As she generally spent a great deal of time in her bedroom, I saw much more of her and I liked that. I no longer barked when anyone entered the room, not much of a guard dog me, but then I could not hear any more. I should have enjoyed a few more years of this pleasant retirement if it had not been for the events which took place that evening.

It was one of those cold and misty evenings that are so unbalancing when you are deaf. Mum had been given permission to use the golf course to walk us dogs, once the players had finished for the day. She decided to give us a much enjoyed run there. There was a garden gate which led directly on to the course and we bunched up, waiting for it to be opened, quivering with anticipation. It was by far our favourite walk.

Because very few dogs were allowed there, the wild life was profuse: there were rabbits galore, families of foxes and, situated right outside the gate, a badgers' sett. Any sensible dog knows not to interfere with a badger, let alone venture down into the sett itself. I had learned that myself as a youngster. It is strictly a job for a professional as Toby, if he had still been around, would have told us. But Barney, as usual, thought he knew best and several times had had to be rescued, twice by the Fire Brigade. Unlike me, he had so far been lucky enough not to run into a badger underground but, all the same, Mum now thought it safer to keep him on a lead until we were well clear of the gate. As usual that evening, we walked over the course past the pond. The Norfolks dashed in and out of the woods, probably yapping frenziedly – one sound I was not sorry to lose. I kept as close to Mum as I could. My sense of smell was as keen as ever and there was still much to enjoy.

I am not entirely sure of what happened next. One moment I was beside Mum, the next I was alone, disorientated, in the cold and the fog. She must have gathered up the other dogs before returning with a torch to look for me, at first on foot and then later in the car. Meanwhile, lost, but not completely down-hearted, I found a hole in the fence. From there I could see light from the lanterns that line Ham Gate Avenue. It was a way home I knew well. As I walked down the side of the road, stiff and cold now, longing for my warm bed and dinner, I did not hear the sound of the car approaching, nor what must have been a screech of brakes. The mighty blow which sent me flying across the road, the flash of pain, and then blackness were all I knew.

How scornful Jessie would have been! How she would have ticked me off! I cannot count the number of times she said it to me, 'There are no second chances with cars. So many of my friends have been squashed out there. You only have to look at the number of dead wild animals you see lying by the side or in the middle of the road.' And now it was my turn.

All that night my body lay wrapped in the tartan car rug and by morning Alastair had arrived. Tenderly they carried my poor remains and buried me next to Tessa and Flora. I watched curiously as they lowered me into a grave dug by Steve the gardener, deep in the ground. I could not help wondering if the foxes would dig me up but, as Steve had dug deeper and deeper, he had said in his beautiful Scottish voice, 'The foxes won't get him now.'

Later, Alastair had the most wonderful headstone made to mark my grave and on it was engraved the following epitaph:

Copper

1983–1998

In loving memory of the professor
A true gentleman of the road,
Tragically removed from our midst
By cruel fate but never to be forgotten
As the poet has said,
'They are not dead who live in hearts
They leave behind.'

So there we are, now you know all about me and although you cannot see me any more I can see you, and it's not so bad up here. I have found Flora and Tessa, Toby, Jessie and Jasper and I have had news of my mother, who is on her way to see me now. What is more, for the first time I can see another of my puppies prancing round Ham Common. He is big, much bigger than me, and black. I remember his mother, a labrador I used to meet secretly in Kingston. How do I know he's mine? His eyes of course. They are my eyes; I would know them anywhere. I shall watch his progress with interest because, from where I am, you can see all and hear all.